JOHN WEST

The Sociology of
Education

Santiago Canyon College

Kendall Hunt
publishing company

Kendall Hunt
publishing company

www.kendallhunt.com
Send all inquiries to:
4050 Westmark Drive
Dubuque, IA 52004-1840

ISBN 978-1-4652-4519-9

Printed in the United States of America
10   9   8   7   6   5   4   3   2   1

Dedication

To my phenomenal granddaughter, Drakey, who, perseveres beyond all expectations.

Contents

Acknowledgements

A profound thank you to the people who did so much to aid me in this project: Lara Sanders, Amanda Smith, and Abby Davis at Kendall Hunt Publishing; Barbara Sproat and Leah Freidenrich at SCC Library for giving me a hand with bibliography; my wife, Suzanne for her patience during this project; my daughter Semara, who helped with graphics and formatting; and Elizabeth Elchlepp, SCC English professor, for sticking to her unrelenting principles in the editing process.

About the Author

John Raymond West was born in Birmingham, Alabama in 1931. He attended public schools there until 1949, when he joined a segregated U. S. Marine Corps in New York. He spent eighteen months in combat in South and North Korea, then having R & R in Kobe, Japan. He returned to the United States at Christmas, 1951, whereupon, he began his college education as a thirty-one year old freshman.

Because of an insular existence during childhood, one devoid of excessive contact with discriminatory practices, his first awareness of blatant racism was in the marines. The capstone of that revelation came in Japan as the result of his off-duty relationship with a Chinese family that was subjected to ethnic discrimination by the Japanese, much the same as the plight of African Americans in the U. S., though not as harsh. That experience revealed to the author that social inequity is universal. Only the factions involved are different.

This deepening interest in, and curiosity about, the consequences of social status differences, and also about the role of access to resources on life chances, led to the focus of education as a major vehicle for upward mobility.

After earning the bachelor's degree from California State University in Fullerton in 1969, and the master's in 1970, West began a journey of forty-three years as a professor of Anthropology and Sociology. He earned the doctorate in education from Nova Southwestern University in 1975.

In seeking to answer some of the questions regarding access to resources, it seemed plausible to expect that a collaboration between the two disciplines of sociology and education might divulge useful insight into the subject of access.

Other publications by the author include the first and second editions of *There Are Always Blue Skies, Over the Dark Clouds, 2006, 2009.*

Part One

Introduction: The Melding of Sociology and Education

Inexhaustible literature exists on the subject of Sociology of Education. What makes this book unique is the impact of contemporary social change on the American educational system. Since social change is ever accelerating, that which excited and inspired us in the past pales by comparison to modern social dynamics. Inherent in any social change is its impact on the various social groups that comprise U. S. society.

Sociology involves the characteristics, interactions, relative positioning and statuses of the social groups within a society. Some of the more salient and most often studied special interest groups in our society are gender, race, ethnicity, age, religion, politics, and social class. The ultimate fate of any of the social groups is, to a great extent, explicitly related to and dependent upon their access to and treatment by the educational systems. The focus of this book is on the extent to which social and cultural changes are factors affecting that access and treatment, and, by extension, the impact on a group's life chances.

Education in the United States, at all levels, is in a defensive mode today. While there does not seem to be a single definitive explanation for the plight of one of the more significant institutions in U. S. society, a reasonable hypothesis might suggest that there is a symbiotic relationship between social institutions and social groups. Neither exists in a vacuum. As society moves along through the evolutionary scheme, each element of it changes at its own pace while influenced by all other elements. "Culture Lag," a concept coined by William Ogburn, 1922/1938, suggests that all facets of society do not change at the same rate (Bryjak and Soroka 66).

Education, by definition, is the intergenerational transmission of knowledge deemed important to and by each society and, therefore, to and by all elements of society. How this is accomplished depends, in large part, upon the nature of the society. Some societies are basically homogeneous throughout, while many, such as the United States, are multicultural, which is the compilation of many subcultures requiring scores of educational delivery strategies to meet each group's needs.

Over the past fifty years, the United States has experienced several major social changes, many of which emanate from the World War Two era. None of these changes have occurred in isolation. With each change in other social institutions, the nature of education and its role has also necessarily evolved. As a result, the vexing problem of educational institutions often seems to be that they are unable to keep abreast of contemporary societal needs. Traditional education is a major player in the concept of cultural lag. When cultural change occurs, education seems to be the slowest of all institutions, including religion, to make the necessary adjustments.

Tradition is a two-edged sword. It can make for phenomenal levels of stability. But it can also be a drag on innovation and creativity. By the time the institution of education is prepared to make required adjustments to the demands of society, new needs will have developed, needs that must now find their place in line for opportunities to be served. The enduring question remains: "Will education ever catch up?"

In the meantime, with diminishing resources available for social programs, the waiting lines get longer. If history is a good indicator, different social groups will be served differently, and unequally, thus, the premise upon which this book is written.

The author's perspective is one based upon experience teaching sociology for forty-three years, with a doctoral degree in education granted in 1975. The melding of these two disciplines has developed a natural curiosity about the importance and relevance of one field to the other. They maintain a symbiotic relationship that is deeper than both would probably prefer to admit. The object, here, is to dispel the notion that the relationship is minimal and to explore ways of exposing the undeniable mutual dependence that has the potential to enhance both.

This discussion will draw upon the voluminous research in the field to supplement "breaking news" regarding current practices in American education. As with all other aspects of society, social change is pervasive. To different degrees, the impact of education both influences and is influenced by all social factors. Key among considerations affecting these influences are timing, perceived needs, availability of resources, and opportunity. The deeper we explore this phenomenon, the more obvious the importance of education and its institutions to the well-being of society.

Diana Kendall, author of *Sociology in Our Times*, says that "Education … is the institution responsible for the systematic transmission of knowledge, skills, and cultural values within a formally organized structure" (Kendall 341). James M. Henslin defines education thusly: "Education is a group's formal system of teaching knowledge, values, and skills" (Henslin 476). He makes the distinction between formal education and acculturation, which simply means learning a culture. Education, as Henslin perceives it, "was intended to develop the mind." This is not meant to disdain "learning a culture," for such was the primary survival strategy for tribal societies and continues to be so for some farming societies. Industrial societies no longer expect that children will learn at the feet of their parents. In 1837, Horace Mann, a Massachusetts educator, developed the concept of "common schools," which were supported by taxes. By 1918, all U.S. states had education supported by taxes and mandatory education laws, which required children to receive formal education up to an age determined by the state based upon the needs and sovereignty of the state. Not all formal education in the U. S., however, is public education. The myriad of alternative approaches has developed in recent times. These will be discussed in later chapters.

Part Two

Sociology: The Study of Group Dynamics

To appreciate the impact of sociology on education, it is necessary to understand the nature of sociology – its origins, its purposes, and the key figures responsible for its founding. The discipline, while sharing with other social sciences the key characteristic of being people oriented, derives its uniqueness from its emphasis on relationships between and among groups, "groups" being the operant word. The issues typically revolve around relative status and power. This is a significant departure from the focus of other social sciences. A close cousin to sociology is the field of psychology, which is more directly concerned with the individual, rather than group dynamics. Sociology deals most commonly with inequities among the variety of social groups.

The other social sciences, including anthropology, political science, economics, history, and geography, all study people, though their approaches are diverse. For example, anthropology, by its rather generic definition, is the "Study of Man." Its specific fields, however, are Cultural, Physical, Linguistics, Archeological, and Applied, each field influenced by the evolutionary process. Political science is about power relationships, which is directly related to group relationships in sociology. Economics is about the production, distribution, and consumption of goods and services. Every facet of these disciplines begins and ends with people. Groups are comprised of people, and people find themselves stationed at different strata accompanied by varying degrees of opportunities. This is the essence of sociology.

Five key theorists, from different perspectives, established sociology as an academic discipline. Their varying orientations, which were only partially reconciled, provided the groundwork for what was to become a major social science—one that touched and was touched by the other social sciences as well as other academic disciplines.

The founder of sociology, also called the father of sociology, was Auguste Comte (1798–1857). Comte's interest in the nature of social order was prompted by social upheaval in Europe, specifically the French Revolution. He began to wonder about the origins of chaos in society and about the ingredients necessary for social order. His thinking was that we could no longer analyze social forces as we had previously. It would be necessary to utilize a method more substantial than what he termed "Armchair Philosophy." (Henslin 10). He proposed the "Scientific Method" for Sociology, which involved the same strategies used in conducting natural science investigation. Such approaches would render the same level of replication as natural scientific research, thus, affording it the same level of credibility. Although Comte was not known for his own field research, he did gain preeminence for proposing a new, more scientific form of conducting research.

Comte felt that sociologists should not only effect social change via the scientific method, but also be involved in implementing that change. Who, he argued, is better suited to improve society than those who know people. Social scientists should be the most people-oriented of all scientists.

A professional contemporary of his, Herbert Spencer (1820–1903), agreed with Comte on the concept of the "Scientific Method"; however, he disagreed with him on getting involved with how research results should be used. His idea was that, yes, social scientists should develop new knowledge (the very definition of research), but should then remove themselves from the equation and allow others to determine how the knowledge should be used. He felt that not to remove one's self is the foundation for bias in resulting research conclusions.

Removing oneself also allows "the chips to fall as they may." Although often attributed to Charles Darwin, Spencer coined the term "Survival of the Fittest," a concept often debated on the subject of life chances and the distribution of power. His belief was that outside forces should not interfere with the natural progression of social dynamics. According to this thinking, the strong would survive and the weak would die off. The consequence, he concluded, would yield a more robust society. This is a time-worn debate, to the point of being threadbare, for it can be heard almost daily in our contemporary political discourse. It is a debate being waged almost daily in the author's sociology and cultural anthropology classes.

Both Comte and Spencer were functionalists. Social functionalism concerns itself not only with how the various parts of society work, but also with how they work in concert for the good of the whole of society. Our focus, here, is to determine the effect of synthesizing the institutions of society and education, and the extent they work together for the good of the society.

A third important social theorist, one who emphasized establishing sociology as a separate academic discipline, was Emile Durkheim (1858–1917). In his work *The Rules of Sociological Method* (1964a/1895), Durkheim concluded that individuals do not function in a vacuum, but, instead, are influenced by their environments. He felt that "*Social Facts* are patterned ways of acting, thinking, and feeling that exist outside any one individual but that exert social control over each person" (Kendall. D.11). Durkheim was also a functionalist, who believed that the whole is far more important than its individual parts. Individuals subconsciously receive their cues from those around them, whether those cues are positive or negative. When they cease to be influenced by outside forces, they fall into a state of what Durkheim referred to as *anomie*. This *state* occurs when individuals sever ties with significant other persons or groups. Durkheim focused much of his work on deviance, concluding that when individuals are in a state of *anomie*, they are far more likely to commit deviant acts.

Durkheim wrote in *Suicide* (1964b/1897) that anomie is "a condition in which social control becomes ineffective as a result of the loss of shared values and a sense of purpose in society" (Kendall 11). His famous influential work concluded that the closer religious denominations embraced their members, the lower the suicide rate. Similarly, married individuals and females also had lower suicide rates. His conclusion was that having significant ties and responsibility for others were deterrents to suicide.

The fourth significant social scientist, who was actually an economist and philosopher, was Karl Marx (1818–1883). Unlike Comte, Spencer, and Durkheim, Marx was a conflict theorist. All of his works reflect conflict and contention. He contends that conflict in society is inevitable due to social classes. Without social classes, he contends, there would be no social conflict. The problem with his theory is that since hunter and gathering societies existed, there has been no evidence of classless societies. It seems that conflict in societies is inevitable, but not necessarily due to social classes. As societies grew in size and complexity, social classes became more and more a part of the social order. The transformation from hunting and gathering to horticultural, pastoral, agricultural, industrial and biotechnical societies witnessed growth in the class system with each new level of technology and the ability for some individuals to wield power over others. So, though social class is an important reason for disparities in society, other factors, such as social values and practices, may have impact as well.

Differing with Marx on the source of social conflict was our fifth social scientist, Max Weber (1864–1920). Weber argued that conflict in society was inevitable, but thought that the source of conflict was religion. Weber wrote a major paper, entitled "The Protestant Ethic and the Spirit of Capitalism," which outlined the parallel developments of Protestantism and capitalism. In it, he compared the fundamentally different belief-systems of Roman Catholics and Protestants. Catholics were told that their passport into heaven was assured if they did good deeds and were kind to their neighbors. On the other hand, Protestants were convinced that although they would not know if they were to be admitted into heaven until judgment day—that judgment would, most likely, be based upon whether or not they were valued by God as indicated by the accumulation of financial success. According to Weber, this was the birth of capitalism, because the accumulation of resources was far more likely to occur among Protestants than Catholics.

Two other concerns of Max Weber were (1) the belief that bureaucracies and their emphasis on routine administration were destructive to human vitality and freedom (13) and (2) that women's issues were more important than most of the social theorists of the day acknowledged. Perhaps his awareness at least partially results from the fact that his wife, Marianne Weber, was an important figure in the women's movement in Germany in the early twentieth century (Kendall 14).

Regardless of these illustrious men, with varied sociological orientations, they were joined with contemporaries who were instrumental in growing the discipline. And, they were not all men. There was a level of sexism in sociology, which originally was dominated by men. But then along came such women as Jane Addams (1860–1935), most noted for co-founding Hull House in Chicago's slums, along with Ellen Gates Starr. In fact, before Durkheim and Weber were born, British sociologist, Harriet Martineau (1802–1876) embellished Comte's work and did a comparative analysis of societies in Great Britain and America. She wrote *Society in America (1962/19837)*, based upon extensive travel and conversation throughout what was then a fledgling United States (Kendall 10).

Other noted social activists included W.E.B Dubois (1868–1963), who wrote *The Philadelphia Negro: A Social Study* (1961), but in modern times is most noted for his book *The Souls of Black Folk* (1903). In it, he depicted the poverty in the lives of Blacks in the 1800's South.

Martineau, Dubois, and other social activists of the time were fixated on the social inequity that permeated society, especially gender and racial inequality. Interestingly, traces of that inequality still exist today, though the extent and form are different. DuBois was so discouraged with the lack of progress regarding social issues in the United States that he moved to Ghana at the age of ninety-three, where he was buried (Henslin 18).

The glue that holds societies together is their institutions, which are formalized organizations that over time have proven to be beneficial to societies. The proof of their importance lies in the extent to which they serve to perpetuate society over vast periods of time. Institutions typically develop through experimentation and the process of determining if they are positive or detrimental for societies' well-being. If, after serious, prolonged consideration, they are deemed to be worthy, their rules and regulations are (1) reduced to writing, in the form of policies, and (2) provided the necessary resources to sustain the policies. At that point new procedures become institutionalized.

Among important institutions in American society are family, law, religion, military, business, politics, economics, and, from this author's perspective, education. Why such a lofty assessment of education, an entity so beset by criticism from basically all of the other institutions? Or to be fair, why are the other institutions looked upon with jaundiced eye by education?

Part Three

Education and Women

Education's significance in the equation of social mobility cannot be overstated. However, each of society's institutions is significant. Otherwise, they would not be institutions. Each contributes to a healthy society in its own way. The functionalist perspective insists that each part of the whole is absolutely essential for the integrity of the whole. Alone, it is insignificant. But grouped together, they are what constitute the integrity of the whole. Obviously, the functionalists had it right. For as we examine any social institution alone, we see immediately how ineffectual it is without benefit and dependence on and collaboration with all of the other major institutions. As with people, each thrives on interdependence with others for its own good health.

Imagine the absence of any one of the major institutions in U.S. society. In spite of provincialism and vitriol, even the most partial thinker would have difficulty reconciling a fragmented, disjointed society. So, all institutions are necessary, and all touch and are touched by all others. A major issue to be emphasized here is the impact of education on not only the other institutions but also the various social factions that comprise U. S. society. This issue is all about the integrity of the whole.

Of the several special interest and perhaps most maligned social groups in American society, females stand out as the most prominently recognized as second–class citizens on every front. Theirs is a more subtle and insidious treatment, for they are often recognized as members of the dominant male category, due to a rather fragile co-dependency relationship. "Sleeping with the enemy" tends to give one a false sense of partnership, parity and security. And, so, when citing disenfranchised groups in America, the tendency is to focus first on race and ethnicity, designations that have been discussed and vilified throughout the country's history. However, the subtlety of gender differences can be both mystifying and discriminatory in a society that claims to offer equal opportunities to all. Certainly the subject of racial and ethnic disparity is ever present, and many skeptics declare it to be an insoluble issue. The matter of sexism, however, has seemed to glide under the radar. And yet in today's America, perhaps due to heightened levels of awareness, gender disparity seems to attract increasing degrees of attention.

The social status and mobility of females in U.S. society, as with all other groups, relates to and depends upon, among other factors, access to educational opportunities. Many components contribute to successful status maintenance and upper mobility, not the least of which is the academic training that prepares individuals for leadership roles and heightened self-concept. Formal education plays a significant role in providing for that need. Education does not guarantee economic riches or successful careers. But it does offer the best chance of success. West (10) postulates that each person is provided with inborn standards, which she or he continually strives to achieve and maintain. The struggle is never-ending, and individuals do not achieve contentment until those standards are met.

While the first wave of the women's movement focused on voting rights, the second wave addressed equal opportunities in the workplace. In both instances, there was growing recognition that knowledge and total emersion in society's important institutions were key to sharing in the responsibility for how social institutions functioned. Awareness and participation depended significantly on institutions that dispensed knowledge. That knowledge is increasingly viewed as the pathway to inclusion in the decision-making process, which ultimately has led to the third wave of the women's movement: 1. replacing men's values in the workplace with women's values, 2. addressing issues of concern for women in the least industrialized nations, and 3. bringing attention to matters involving women's sexual pleasure. As one can see, all three movements revert back to the first. They all deal with injustices borne of basic men's values. Education leads us to wonder if society's emphasis on theoretical men's values is serving society as well as the alternative of theoretical women's values. History has taught us that some adjustment in our approaches to management and governance might be in order. There appears to be increasing interest in modes that allow for cooperation and negotiation in the decision-making process.

In viewing women's roles in the United States from the beginning of the 20th century, each decade has revealed a correlation between the nature of the roles and the influence of educational access. When the primary goal of the initial women's movement in the 1920's was to seek the right to vote, it demanded education to provide an informed female base. The traditional role of females in the United States began with the notion that leadership responsibilities rested with men, especially with regards to family dynamics, which spilled over into other aspects of social institutions. Even today, in spite of progress in the world of work, inequity in advancement opportunities remains, which translates into the all-important earning capacity based upon gender. The gender-gap in earnings continues to be appalling in a society that proclaims itself to be enlightened and on the leading edge of progress and change on the international scene.

One wonders how a society can reconcile a pay-gap of twenty-three percent, with women earning seventy-seven cents for every dollar earned by men in 2009 (8). That gap has persisted in spite of gains in women's earnings from 1980 to 1990. But the gains have decreased between 1990 and 2000 (CONSAD 4). The dreadfully low percentage of women CEO's in the Fortune 500 is telling. The numbers vacillate between ten to twelve women CEO's out of five hundred. And then notice that generally the types of corporations they lead are women and children's products. BREAKING NEWS! General Motors at this writing has appointed its first female CEO, Mary Barra. Forty-two percent of General Motor's Board of Directors is also female. Is there any connection? This is significant, since fifty Fortune Five Hundred corporations have no female directors.

So, why has each decade presented differential opportunities for women socially, economically, and politically? A popular rebuttal to the call for corrective action to ameliorate the disparity in gender-based earnings is the notion that the disparity is not based upon gender discrimination at all, but instead, on additional factors, such as choices made by women due to a different value system. The emphasis (on job status and earning capacity) tends to be more important to males than to females. But that notion may be more related to societal values than strictly to the values of males in U.S. society. It is interesting that much of the research deals solely with the numbers and not with the causes of the differential in earning capacities of U.S. males and females.

A key official in the U.S. Department of Labor, Charles E. James, Jr., Deputy Assistant Secretary for Federal Contract Compliance, has contended that "the differences in raw wages may be almost entirely the result of the individual choices being made by both male and female workers." James argues in the foreword of a CONSAD report to the U. S. Department of Labor (CONSAD 2) "that there may be no need for corrective action. There may be nothing to correct." The gender disparity that exists today in pay rates and career opportunities would indicate that there is, indeed, serious need for corrective action. Beyond the hunting and gathering era, the history of work in the United States has always positioned women in subservient roles. The disparity reached its peak at the dawn of the agricultural stage.

Harriet Martineau (1802–1876) wrote:

> *The intellect of woman is confined by an unjustifiable restriction. . . . As women have none of the objects in life which an enlarged education is considered requisite, the education is not given . . . [s]ome things [are] taught which . . . serve to fill up time . . . to improve conversation, and to make women something like companions to their husbands, and able to teach their children somewhat . . . There is rarely or never a . . . promotion of their intellectual activity . . . [a]s long as women are excluded from the objects for which men are trained . . . intellectual activity is dangerous: or, as the phrase is, unfit. Accordingly marriage is the only object left open to women. (Henslin 19)*

So, what would be the need for education for women in their 1800's traditional role? As we have marched through each decade since Martineau, "baby steps" have been accomplished with regards to women's progress in access to educational and career opportunities. James's remark that "there may be nothing to correct" borders on the ludicrous, since a progressive disparity in wages is a matter of common knowledge (1). In order to justify corrective action, it must first be acknowledged that a problem exists.

Discussions about the difference in wages between men and women reveal numerous causes for the disparity, not the least of which are the choices made by women. It is legendary that women have had the proclivity to emphasize domestic responsibilities over activities outside the home. However, along with the evolution of gender roles in the United States (especially since World War II), women focus more on interests that are more highly regarded by the society. The interests more ascribed to men have dominated the preoccupation of the society as a whole. A primary consideration regarding role status, from the earliest societies, has been the extent to which individuals (men and women) have contributed to the economic interests of the family. The domestic interests, to the detriment of society, have been routinely relegated to a subservient position in the hierarchy.

The right to vote necessitated the appreciation of not only its importance but also its intricacies. Informal education, education resulting simply from observing the power dynamics in society, is increasingly indicative of how the game was played. Formal education, which is played out with established educational institutions, was another matter. Males have extraordinary access to, and perceived need for, formal education. After all, what better way to negotiate the machinations of progress and upward mobility? And who most has the need for career and financial progression, primarily because men were, indeed, the breadwinners for the family? Women, it was supposed, had no such need for progression, for their domestic roles did not require special skills. In fact, for women, education could be considered dangerous. The prevailing dictum of keeping women "barefoot and pregnant" set the tone for the acquisition of formal education.

There have been both social and institutional gains for women's educational opportunities. Though they may seem to be sparse, they are significant in that they opened the door to career chances. Those gains were spawned not only by advocacy groups, but also by governmental organizations prompted by the ground swell of basic dissatisfaction with gender inequity among the nation's women. The American Association of University Women (AAUW), for example, has been a prime mover in the cause of women's educational opportunities. Its efficacy perhaps was precipitated by introduction of the U. S. government's policy in Title IX of the Education Amendments Act of 1972. That Act states that "No person in the United States shall, on the basis of sex, be excluded from participation in, be denied the benefits of, or be subjected to discrimination under any education program or activity receiving federal financial assistance" (11). Enforced by both the U. S. Department of Education and the federal Office of Civil Rights, the Act, for one very important point, made it necessary for females to receive financial support commensurate with men. A key element of this requirement involved equal treatment in the area of sports and athletics, which had been a glaring inequity for as long as such activities have been of value.

The added value was not perceived to rest solely in physical activity, but in the long-term benefits of participation in valued athletics, such as those involving males, which are most often attended and which are likely to sell the most tickets. While these tend to be important considerations, others may be less likely to be identified, but likely to provide more long-term benefits. Often overlooked, the first of these benefits are athletic scholarships, which are disproportionately meted out to male athletes. For many students, scholarships are the ticket to college. Although both students and institutions sometimes abuse these scholarship systems, these scholarships can, and often do, provide legitimate educational opportunities for serious student athletes. Absolutely nothing is ever totally without flaws. To get to college, and to matriculate, may ultimately provide the means to progress in areas previously unimagined (such as public relations and other fields associated with name recognition). While such progression is sometimes questionable, without the educational experience, such progression would be all but impossible. Both the deserving and the undeserving get a shot at success in the world of work. What they do with those opportunities will depend upon individual efforts.

Education is a prime mover in upward mobility for all segments of society, whether the segment is based on gender, race and ethnicity, social class, or age. Acknowledging the relative importance of education to access power and control is crucial to empowerment, for progress begins by analyzing one's position in society and deciding what must be done to improve that position. Women's progression through the years has always coincided with first acknowledgement of the imbalance, and then the resolve to mitigate the situation. All roads ultimately lead to (and from) education. This recognition is what has propelled women, as with other disenfranchised groups, to use education as the vehicle to all manner of social success.

To understand how we arrived at our present position, it is necessary to review the history of the evolution of the dynamic between the plight of women in the United States and how the predicament has been influenced by the institution of American education. The interaction between the two has not always been compatible. In fact, according to the U.N. Development Program, 1995, women are overrepresented among the world's poor (Pearce, D. 28–36). Commiserate with that situation is the placement of women among the least educated around the globe. The relationship between earnings and educational attainment by sex is extremely significant. The many factors that restrict potential for career or professional advancement seem embedded in historical perceptions of appropriate gender roles in U.S. society. Those perceptions have monumental impact on who most requires and benefits from formal education. Educational levels influence earning capacity. But earning capacity differs significantly based upon gender (See Bureau of Statistics, U.S. Department of Labor chart.) Note, though women have fared better than men with respect to earnings growth over the 1979 to 2002 period, the differential between men's versus women's earnings at every educational level has been constant.

As reflected in the above chart, disparity shows up in two significant ways. Earning capacity was substantially less for women with less than a high school diploma than those with college degrees. So, a college education, though less valuable for women than for men, is more profitable regardless to gender. The matter of access to education in general and higher education in particular makes the difference between self-sufficiency and dependency. As this has become more and more obvious to women, the clamor for educational opportunities has ramped up with each generation. Also evident in the chart is the more promising statistic indicating that with the passage of time both women and men have lost ground in earning capacity. However, women have lost less ground than men. In the same span of time, women's educational levels have increased proportionally to earning advancements.

In a society such as the U.S., where the accumulation of resources is highly valued, earning capacity is crucial. Unfortunately, individual worth is gauged by material assets, assets that are very closely tied to one's ability to acquire material and non-material possessions. Such assets are very often self-propagating. Assets have the tendency to expand, very often with little effort, such as with property appreciation. Property comes in many forms, as with copyrights, patents, and lucrative titles, in addition to material property. Educational experiences are most often functional in achieving such assets. Only in the most unusual circumstances are individuals likely to accumulate such assets without at least a moderate level of formal education. Individuals with few discretionary assets have little opportunity to expend resources in other than the bare necessities to sustain life. Not only have women had little opportunity to acquire and maintain such holdings on their own, but also historically they have too often been regarded as property by men (Henslin 292). However, positive changes have occurred over the past five decades. An easily defensible explanation could be the generational progression of women's access to education at all levels. Eventually it became recognized that education and general awareness are what have sustained men in the society throughout history, especially with regards to trade, travel, and communication with outside groups. Being restricted to the hearth provides none of these experiences, which translate to opportunities.

The ratio of women's earnings compared to men's vacillates between 70 cents on the dollar to 76 cents, depending on the source. If there is any promising note about these figures, it is that in 1970 the ratio was 61 cents on the dollar, which means that things are moving in the right direction. However, given the history of comparative earnings, one has to wonder if the gap will ever close completely. Some consideration must be given that there are circumstances contributing to the discrepancy that will be difficult to overcome, such as lower earnings being acceptable to women who see outside work to be secondary to homemaking and childcare. And there is the issue of women not having access to career mentors to the extent that men do.

Bureau of Labor Statistics, U.S. Department of Labor, *The Editor's Desk*, Earnings by educational attainment and sex, 1979 and 2002 on the Internet at http://www.bls. gov/opub/ted/2003/oct/wk3/art04.htm (visited *October 17, 2013*).

Median weekly earnings of full-time wage and salary workers by educational attainment and sex, 1979 and 2002

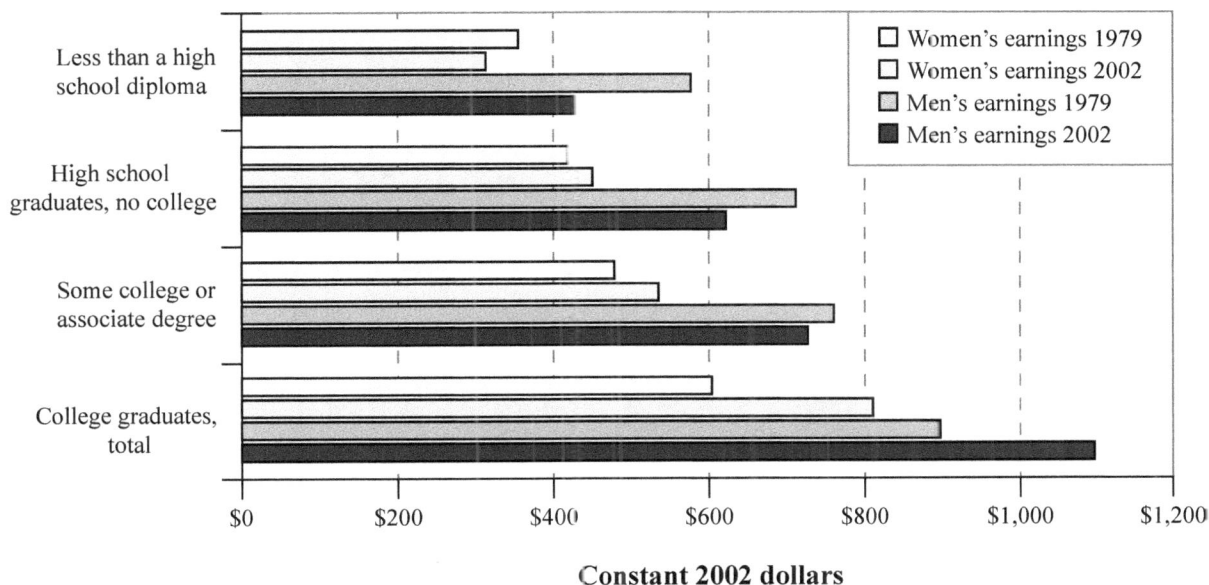

Constant 2002 dollars

Women with less than a high school diploma earned $323 per week in 2002, compared with $809 for those with a college degree.

Among men, high school dropouts had earnings of $421 a week, compared with $1,089 for college graduates.

At all levels of education, women have fared better than men with respect to earnings growth over the 1979 to 2002 period.

Although both women and men with less than a high school diploma have experienced a decline in inflation-adjusted earnings since 1979, women's earnings have fallen significantly less—from $348 to $323 (down 7.2 percent), compared with a 27.2 percent drop from $578 to $421 for men.

Earnings for women with college degrees have increased by one-third from $605 to $809 since 1979 on an inflation-adjusted basis, while those of male college graduates have risen by only one-fifth from $908 to $1,089.

These data come from the *Current Population Survey*. For more information, see "*Highlights of Women's Earnings in 2002*," BLS Report 972 (PDF 188K). Earnings data in this article are annual average median usual weekly earnings of full-time wage and salary workers 25 years of age and older expressed in constant 2002 dollars.

Part Four

The Interweaving of Race and Ethnicity with Education

Too often, the concepts of race and ethnicity are confused and used interchangeably. While the two may have many characteristics in common, they are notably different concepts. One might argue that the two are evolving in two different directions with regards to importance in American society. Any definition of race necessarily includes either "biological" or "physical" traits. The significance of such traits has decreased in major ways in the society because of the blurring of the differences due to the admixture of racial types. Social contact and interracial marriages are on the increase. Globalization has increased physical and social contact among groups around the world. Racial phenotypes are more and more indistinguishable due to group mobility and less distinguishable climate change over vast amounts of time. Consider, for example, the effects of global warming on the environment and its consequences for geographic determinism on groups' physical characteristics. It has become increasingly difficult to categorize individuals by race on the basis of their physical appearance. Conventional wisdom might suggest that we withhold judgment, for identification purposes, based upon their appearance. And yet, errors of this sort are committed daily primarily because the tendency is to take the path of least resistance by simply categorizing all people who look similar into the same group. Unless, and until, society decides that this practice is foolhardy, embarrassments of this kind will continue. The hope is that sophistication and awareness will gradually make such practices uncommon.

The question of whether or not race is of importance in U.S. society produces elusive responses. There continues to be talk of a "post-racism" society. Such a concept would indicate that we are beyond concerns of inequity based on race. Some have even suggested that the focus is more on "class distinctions," as opposed to race. Sociologist William Julius Wilson, for example, has concluded that our fundamental issue today is not one of race, but one of social class. Wilson states that "it is not an either-or question. My book is titled *The **Declining** Significance of Race*," he would say, "not *The **Absence** of Race*. Certainly racism is still alive," he would add, "but today social class is more central to the African American experience than is racial discrimination. He stresses that we need to provide jobs for the poor in the inner city—for work provides an anchor to a responsible life (Wilson 1996, 2007). The concept of race has seemed to take a back seat to social class among many African Americans, as evidenced by the tendency of the different social classes to relate to and interact more with people of the same social class than with those who simply share the same racial characteristics. This is significant because African Americans have been victimized and influenced by how they were perceived by others, especially Whites. So as African Americans loosen the reins of self-denigrating perceptions, the influence of others will tend to degrade commensurate with the passage of time.

While Wilson offers a tempting argument, much information belies the very basis of his notion. A major discrepancy is the disparity in pay between African Americans, both male and female. The matter of both de jure and de facto segregation in housing carries over to below average community schools and educational opportunities, which translate into limited career opportunities. In addition, major differences in access to health care translate into disproportionate mortality rates. It may sound sensible to expect the different social strata among African Americans to associate primarily with their kind. But this also leads to groups being concerned only with their kind. There is a history of middle- and upper-class African Americans drawing a clear line between themselves and those who were less fortunate (a condition which still exists among some and certainly among some other racial and ethnic groups). It took far too long for all African Americans to realize that they were all in the same boat. A basic premise suggests that people who are discriminatory and prejudiced against one group are likely to be so towards all groups unlike themselves, though perhaps to different degrees. Though the level of bias may be disproportionate, the tendency for bigotry is likely to persist.

Any discussion of race in the United States, here, includes all of the racial groups that comprise the society. History has taught us that racism is not simply a Black/White issue. Though expressions of pride in the contributions of the many different immigrant groups are legendary, a parallel, unexpressed sentiment continually indicates that all are not necessarily welcomed and that groups are treated accordingly. And who sets the standards of acceptance? Certainly not the indigenous Native Americans, who are today worse off in every category than all other disenfranchised in the land. They have the lowest rate of life expectancy, fewer of them finish college, they have the highest suicide rate in the nation, and they tend to be treated as the Invisible Minority because of their isolation from other groups. Much of the separatism preferred by many Native Americans relates to the quest for self-control and the unwillingness to join with those whom they perceive to be would-be conquerors.

Discussions of poverty among Native Americans inevitably get around to casino ownership. As the result of many recent court victories, Native Americans do, indeed, own more profitable casinos than all of those in Las Vegas (Pratt 2011, Statistical Abstract 2011: Table 1257). But the 26 billion dollars a year these casinos bring in annually do not tell the whole story. These holdings are owned by a few individuals and tribes. One such tribe has only one member who owns her own casino (Bartlett and Steele 2002). All of the social and economic disparities mentioned above persist in Native American society today. Native Americans are often dismissed as a people who desire to retain their own culture. They have the audacity to perceive themselves as not being a single homogeneous group, but as multiple, unique tribes with their regional and cultural interests. In fact, they are often times thrown in with other minority groups that they physically resemble, regardless of how strongly they may feel about their own idiosyncratic approach to life.

Stereotypes continue to plague them, such as being barbaric and murderous, consumed by "firewater," and insisting on being isolationists. Often forgotten is the intent of the conquering Europeans to totally eradicate Native Americans, not simply remove or isolate them. These efforts failed only because of the resolve of the tribe to resist decimation of their culture and the physical determination to ward off aggression. In addition, Native Americans knew the terrain on their soil better than their invaders. And the all-important factor of pride, which all groups exercise when their space is being intruded upon, motivated Native Americans to survive. This is often what wars are about. Because they dared to fight back, this resistance gave them the reputation of being bloodthirsty and vicious. The resolve to remain an entity of its own continues to present perception problems about, not for, Native Americans today. What must not be forgotten is the contemporary plight of the first Americans.

American society continues to be hampered by the "they all look alike to me" syndrome. They look alike, so they must be alike. This notion has become less and less probable since changes brought about during and after the civil rights movement of the fifties and sixties. That movement brought about a new consciousness first for America's blacks, but also for all other groups in the society. For Blacks, it was the first time "Black is beautiful" became a reality for many in the country. Prior to that movement, Black was seen as anything but beautiful. The rampant self-hate that had existed among African Americans, who received their cues primarily from Whites, was beginning to be challenged by a birth of interest in the relevance of one's own group, not only among African Americans, but other groups as well, including Whites. Outward expressions of racial and ethnic pride, which heretofore had been subdued, were now expressed by a "circling-of-the-wagons" mentality, to boost the significance of one's own group. The license plate covers expressing "pride is being Irish," or "pride is being Italian American" were virtually unheard of prior to the civil rights movement.

Civil rights leader, Whitney Young, Jr., declared that the civil rights movement gave freedom and responsibility to all Americans. As he puts it, "Black is beautiful when it is a slum kid studying to enter college, when it is a man learning new skills for a new job, or a slum mother battling to give her kids a chance for a better life. But white is beautiful, too, when it helps change society to make our system work for black people also. White is ugly when it oppresses blacks—and so is black ugly when black people exploit other blacks. No race has a monopoly on vice or virtue, and the worth of an individual is not related to the color of his skin" (750). Because of the civil rights movement, Whites were free to go on about their own business, further promoting their own already inflated advantages, as opposed to having to hang around to curtail the progress of African Americans. This thinking is partially correct. Much of the damage had already been done to African Americans, who were already situated in an untenable situation. The gap would be difficult to bridge after such an extended period of deprivation.

Young did allow that certain efforts must be exerted to alleviate some of the discrepancies from the past. His activism was in response to criticisms of new programs developed to compensate for past group inequities, such as affirmative action (which is being taken up by the Supreme Court at this writing). The subject of the appropriateness of Affirmative Action has never decreased in controversy since its inception in 1965. The usual impetus for criticisms occurs when a member of the majority population has been rejected for admission at a university or is unsuccessful in a hiring process in favor of a minority person who is suspected of being less qualified. The word "quota" has become an ugly word in American discourse. The fact is that such a concept would never have been necessary if rampant institutionalized discrimination had not been allowed to prevail throughout the nation's history. Most individual court cases challenging affirmative action have been successful. Those cases look at situations on an individual basis, and not the predicament of the class and its history. On the face of such cases, it is simply a matter of right and wrong. The tendency, then, is to over-simplify the matter. The matter today is approaching forty-eight years and shows no sign of going away.

Education, being an acknowledged formal transmitter of information over generations, has had major impact on all interest groups in American society. The impact, though important, has had differential impact on different groups, primarily due to differential access to this vital institution. When Thomas Jefferson and Noah Webster proposed the notion of universal schooling, they were perceiving the concept as a tool to promote patriotism and representative government. One has only to review Jefferson's background to imagine which citizens he had in mind for participation. The proposal was an ideal one with supposedly noble intentions. The experiment did not succeed and inequity and political upheaval continued to exist.

It was not until 1837 that Horace Mann, a Massachusetts educator, proposed what he called common schools, to be supported by taxes. This proposal led to the spread of the concept throughout the country. All U. S. states soon had mandatory education laws, and with their sovereignty, had different requirements, such as age and grade attainment. Such proposals had the potential for uniform national success. If administered uniformly. However, consider the state where the idea was first implemented, and then consider the political landscape throughout the nation, notably the South. What were the chances of all states agreeing that all citizens should be uniformly educated? This condition continues to be with us well into the twenty-first century.

That education has treated different racial and ethnic groups inequitably is common Knowledge. What makes the difference, group-to-group? A number of factors enter into this discussion, not the least of which is a group's placement within the social hierarchy. What is interesting is that such placement is done primarily at the whim of the majority group. Unfortunately, in the past, minority groups have tended to internalize the majority group's perceptions. Fortunately, political activism indicates that the situation is changing somewhat in that regard. Group pride has emerged significantly in the last few decades. Though the society definitely has not rid itself of racism, the matter of ethnicity is sharing the political stage at increasing levels.

While the concept of race concerns itself with differences in biological and physical characteristics, ethnicity involves cultural differences. Ethnicity is about how groups manage to distinguish themselves from others culturally. Groups tend to identify themselves by their languages, foods, clothing, rituals, and families. These conventions run fairly constant for a group, but subject to changes brought about by new imperatives resulting from globalization. The idea of ethnicity has grown in importance in a society that has the exceptional potential for melding of cultural ways. As was mentioned before, American society has had the tendency to use the concepts of race" and "ethnicity" interchangeably, but really seeing ethnicity referring to racial groups. Ethnicity could only be applied to American society and, specifically, to people of color. It was difficult to comprehend the notion of "ethnic cleansing," which was being discussed about Muslims being slaughtered by the Serbs in Bosnia. How could there be ethnic cleansing in Bosnia when there are no Black folks? Slowly, we are coming to understand that ethnicity involves all hues in humans. Even in the United States, unaware people are unfamiliar with a very large proportion of the population defined as "White Ethnics." They not only exist, but also have existed with subjugated status throughout the nation's history. The second group that populated this country, after the Native Americans, was the WASPs, White Anglo Saxon Protestants, who set the standards of acceptance for all who followed. Those who followed were European immigrants who were dissimilar to the WASPs who were already established. The newcomers, though similar in physical characteristics, were different culturally, especially with regards to religion among the Irish. The closer the newcomers came to approximating the WASPs, the more they were accepted. The ideal was to either resemble the WASPs, or to be in the process of becoming like them. So, ethnicity is not unique to Blacks, Browns Yellows, and Reds. The largest group of White Ethnics in the U. S. is of German descent, distantly followed by Irish-Americans.

What, then, has been the significance of education to these diverse groups? Except for a few strains of commonality, the significance has been as diverse as the groups themselves. The group's status in the social hierarchy has played a major part in its acceptance and, therefore, treatment by the more powerful majority. Among the deciding factors is the question of when and how the group joined the society. African Americans have paid a sizable price for their history as slaves. It is difficult to outlive such a long period in servitude of the type they endured. Many of the issues they face today are products of that history. An important effort to keep the subjugated in "their place" was the fairly successful attempt to prevent them from becoming educated. One of the important strains of commonality among all of the disenfranchised groups has been the expressed and sometimes passive attempt to deprive them of access to education.

Denying women access to educational opportunities can easily be interpreted as a scheme for subjugation. The main focus of the deprivation was to keep women out of the mainstream of society. Until recently, it has been safe to declare the society to be a "man's world." The history skews our perception of present-day realities. It continues to be important to recognize that history, for it should serve to ensure that society does not repeat itself. Fortunately, many students today find it difficult to fathom the realities of the 1800's. Dr. Edward Clarke, of Harvard University stated that *"A girl upon whom Nature, for a limited period and for a definite purpose, imposes so great a physiological task, will not have as much power left for the tasks of school, as the boy of whom Nature requires less at the corresponding epoch. (Andersen 1988)* Because women are so much weaker than men, Clarke urged them to study only one-third as much as men. And, of course, in their weakened state, they were not advised to not study at all during menstruation (Henslin 298).

One strategy for keeping women out of the mainstream was the use of a concept called "gender tracking," a process designed to guide them into academic pursuits that were less threatening to men, such as homemaking, childrearing, and other care-giving duties. College majors that were deemed appropriate were in the same vein and included "feminine" roles, such as secretary science, library science, nursing, and, today, human resources. In the meantime, men were "appropriately" involved in manly pursuits, such as engineering, medicine, and law. The consequences produced a gendered workforce that rewarded males and females inequitably. The importance of education begins to reveal why the clamor for education has proliferated to such a great extent in recent years. It does not take a professional degree to understand what is regarded as important in society and what one must do to acquire a position in the hierarchy. Males continue to outdistance females in professional degrees in every field, though the gap has closed considerably in the medical doctor category. Of the sciences, women outnumber men only in the field of psychology, which tends to resemble the feminine fields concerned with family, care, and emotions. A major problem with these fields is that they do not earn massive paychecks. And yet, they may be regarded as some of the most important functions in society. The absence of concern for these fields has put the society in a tentative position. We are one of the few major industrialized nations that does not appreciate that our children's education is critical to our future. Claiming to be on the leading edge of change, American society suffers a glaring discrepancy in gender equity issues. Access to power positions in society relate closely to access to educational experiences. These experiences are the pathway to political and corporate participation. Only in the last few decades have women advanced to important positions in the American political system. Indications are that this is a matter that is fast rectifying itself. Inequity in any direction, however, is unacceptable. One has to wonder what this signifies for the future. Like the phantom concept of post-racism, will there be a post-inequity period?

Of the top Fortune Five Hundred corporations in the U. S., only twelve have women CEO's (Henslin 303). That's twelve out of five hundred. Of the forty-four presidents that have been elected in the U. S., none have been women. Are these appalling numbers accidental? Are there no women who rise to the levels necessary to serve in these leadership roles? Throughout history, forty-nine countries have had female leaders. Currently, only nineteen such nations exist. The United States (remember the leading edge of change?) is not one of them. But the increased numbers of women in legislative and cabinet positions, not to speak of governorships, portends imminent change in the American body politic.

Different aspects of changes in women's status in society do not occur in a vacuum. Major impetus happens as the of result changes in access to educational opportunities. But these changes came about as the result of informal enlightenment due simply to the observation of power dynamics. The result was the recognition that education, among other factors, was a major player in social progression. The discrepancies mentioned in the previous paragraphs were all due to the belief by men, and often by women, that exposure to activities outside the home were not needed by women, for these were men's responsibilities. As we observe the changing dynamics of gender roles in the society, the importance of education in general, and formal education in particular, has become just as necessary for women as for men. More than fifty percent of women work outside the home for wages today. The question becomes "what kind of work?" Professional, managerial, and skilled occupations typically require formal education. Until recently, women did not acquire these experiences in large numbers. The expectation was that men needed such training to carry out their assigned roles. For a long while women were contented with their lot. And then the society experienced major economic changes that required both men and women to contribute to the family fiscal well-being. This was a major game changer, for now both parties became important, which altered interpersonal relationships. The quest for educational opportunities, especially higher education, became crucial for both genders.

Education has not accommodated men and women equally. Even at the elementary level, studies have shown that teachers have different expectations of boys and girls. This is crucial, because both students and pupils tend to attempt to live up to teachers' expectations, whether the expectations are positive or negative. Males are expected to be aggressive and dominant, while females are expected to be docile and passive. The tendency is for teachers to be more responsive to male's inquiries than females'. It is easy to see just how all of this translates to the real world when it comes to the treatment of men and women. Education is a major socializing agent. It has significant influence on how individuals perceive themselves, positively or negatively. Sociologist Charles Horton Cooley's (1864–1929) concept, "Cooley's Looking-Glass Self," explains this influence (Henslin 66). Teachers, coaches, ministers, peers, parents, siblings, and close friends all have major influence on how we perceive ourselves. Education goes a long way in influencing us because of those positive or negative expectations.

The author recounts in the following vignette, from his own experiences, how race and ethnicity form us:

> It's Birmingham, Alabama, (circa the 30's and 40's), a city thought by many to be the most racist in the nation. A city savagely divided between the two major races, Blacks and Whites. A city divided by both de facto and de jure segregation. Jim Crow laws prescribed the lives of all who inhabited the city. Blacks were unabashedly relegated to animal-like existences. And yet families of both hues were expected to do all of the things expected of families with vastly different level

of resources. For the most part, Blacks were abjectly poor, with a few who were other than poor, but not "rich" by Whites' standards. My family, which consisted of my mother, a sister, me, and a sometimes father (and later a step father), was among the poor. It was basically a dysfunctional family, primarily because of the unstable father and stepfather. Both were hard workers who chased women, and squandered their earnings. One was a drunk, and the other was a gambler. Both physically abused my mother, which set the tone for my attitude regarding gender inequity. Mama was an educated woman who graduated from college and was teaching public school at the age of eighteen. She was also a very bitter woman because of the racism and sexism that prevented her from plying her trade as a teacher once it was learned that she was married and had children. Consequently, she wound up working in the homes of Whites who were not as educated as she and could not afford to pay for the work she did. Often she was rewarded with hand-me-downs. Because of the poverty we endured, the homes we lived in were not fit for human habitation. Because there were no public places for recreational swimming for African Americans, young boys swam in swimming holes infested with human excrement from an adjacent steel plant. Few living quarters had indoor toilets and running water. Violence ran rampant in all of the communities, violence that no child should be required to witness.

Healthcare as we know it today was completely nonexistent for this community. No one had a family physician or a health plan. Injuries and illnesses were treated with home remedies, such as spider webs, leaves and salves to draw out infections. Never once did I see a doctor or dentist during childhood, except for five days hospitalization for pneumonia. Mortality rates were extremely high due to contaminants and pollutants from work in the many steel plants.

Strangely enough, education was highly valued for this lower class community, though it is difficult to see why anyone felt that it would get them out of their situation. The emphasis seemed to be especially high for getting women educated. Their career choices were limited, but not so much as men's. Women could get professional work primarily in teaching and nursing. Men were limited even further. Families were predisposed to scrape together their meager resources to get their daughters through college rather than the sons because the promise of meaningful jobs was greater for women. Mothers were known to wear their hands to the bone to get their children to and through the many traditionally African American colleges. The circumstances of preference for women presented problems with the men in interpersonal relationships due to the heighten status of women. In the home, men tended to be subjugated because of their lack of status with regards to educational preparation. So, even in this depressed community, education was very significant.

The above account is a brief glimpse into what poverty looked like in this place, at this time, and with this community. But little is universal about poverty. Though there may be similarities from group to group, each has its own crosses to bear. While this description reflects conditions in an African American community, none of us exists in a vacuum, and because disenfranchised groups are thrown into the same categories socially and economically, there is common understanding about what each group is enduring. What is difficult to comprehend is the intergroup conflict that occurs in spite of that acknowledgement. It is a mentality that existed among African Americans prior to the civil rights movement, when a stratification system among them pitted one stratum against the others based upon personal holdings and how their perception by the majority group. Due to increased awareness that they were all perceived negatively, regardless of educational levels and affluence, that situation has seemed to subside with each passing decade. A comparison of how education has affected each racial and ethnic group will prove to be revealing.

AFRICAN AMERICANS

Much of what has transpired with regards to educational policy changes and the impact on minorities began with African Americans challenging the deplorable status quo. Most other minority groups were not on the scene initially. Problems with segregation in education for other groups had existed, but the protests early on were mild by comparison. Consider, for example, incidents in Westminster and Santa Ana, California, where as late as 1944 Latinos were segregated by race because some people perceived them as lacking hygiene and English skills. Ironically, the infamous Mendez case was filed by the NAACP (National Association for the Advancement of Colored People). Briefs were co-authored and filed by an African American, Civil Rights attorney Thurgood Marshall, who later became Associate Justice of the Federal Supreme Court. Other civil rights organizations later became active in the cause of discrimination, especially in education. The League of United Latino American Citizens (LULAC), which was established in 1930, was a major force in attaining Latino rights in the forties. However, the organization has lost strength recently due to declining membership and decreasing operating funds. Like the NAACP, membership tends to be less active than it was previously. Japanese Americans were also segregated in some Orange County schools until 1945, an interesting phenomenon, since the country was just coming out of war against the Japanese in World War Two, and many were segregated into internment camps. We will come back to Japanese Americans later, but the template established by the African American movement continues to be used by all groups seeing the need for activism today. Early on, it was recognized that without certain disruption in the social order of things, nothing changed. Upon investigation, the pattern of strategies persists, whether concerning racial and ethnic groups, gender issues, or ageism, or social class inequality. All see the need to attract attention before there is even the possibility of progress.

And so, case after case was brought by African Americans, who at the time were the largest racial minority group in the nation. The movement involved far more than filing legal suits. The demonstrations, marches, riots, and on-going protests were promoted and conducted with and by African Americans. In the process of conducting such activities, lives were sacrificed, bodies were maimed, jobs were lost, and educational opportunities were stymied. There was a high price to pay for activism. But due to previous conditions of servitude and pervasive inequity, no price was deemed too high to effect change. Although the losses suffered in these activities were primarily to African Americans, other citizens saw the need for change and became involved, as well. By now, it is commonly known that a number of Caucasians, especially from Northern states but also Southern Whites, were also present in the South and in some cases paid the supreme price for their involvement.

Education tended to indulge the requirements of White students, especially in the South, but to a lesser degree also in the North and West. The author recalls having to read from books that had been discarded by White schools and sitting at desks that were worn and carved with graffiti by White students. Some of the buildings in Birmingham were totally dilapidated and unfit for housing children. The teachers and administrators in what were called "colored" schools were compensated far less than their White counterparts, in spite of being regulated by the same governing board. The emphasis in most Southern African American schools was on other than academics. Athletics and industrial arts were deemed to be more suited for the students' future adult roles. Parker High School, which the author attended, was formally Industrial High (Shades of Booker T. Washington, who felt that Negroes should be trained to work with their hands, rather than with their brains). Washington was anything but an academician. He saw African Americans as farmers, carpenters, shoe cobblers, ironworkers, and such. Many, especially Black schools, in the south took up the charge and oriented their studies to industrial tasks. The real problem with a stubborn position such as Washington's is the inability to see the requirement for both schools of thought. In today's world, we call that critical thinking.

W.E.B. Du Bois, a sociologist, novelist, and journalist was adamantly opposed to Washington's prescription for African American progress. He espoused the need to attain higher education and to seek political office. He saw Washington's efforts as inferior energy. He co-founded the NAACP and was editor of its publication *Crisis*. He is credited with hundreds of writings and important books, including *The Souls of Black Folk* and *The Philadelphia Negro*. His experiences with racism drove him to revolutionary Marxism. In fact, in spite of his many accomplishments, he was not recognized as a serious sociologist in the early stages of his career. In thumbing through sociology textbooks, one will notice that he is seldom mentioned among the founding sociologists. His emphasis on educating the Black masses made him suspect, even among many Blacks.

Perhaps there was valid reason for that suspicion. Washington preceded Du Bois as the preeminent activist in the Black community. His message of conciliation was not met well by many who saw a disconnect between barely making ends meet and making social and economic progress. Washington adopted the concept of what he called "racial uplift." Acquiescence was the byword, which bought into the idea of social segregation, provided that Whites would support Black's progress in areas he perceived to be important, the most crucial of which was agriculture. Both Washington and Du Bois were accomplished political tacticians. Washington promised something for everyone. Blacks would receive the resources to gain access to ownership of businesses and land. Whites would be guaranteed a subservient, contented work force that knew and appreciated "their place." In later years, Washington would be dismissed simply as an "Uncle Tom." But his orientation should be considered in context of the times.

Minor advancements had been accomplished by the time Du Bois arrived on the scene, so that progressive thought was in order. A more recalcitrant Black population was beginning to emerge. Most generational movement in African American progression has been initiated and sustained by younger people. The younger ones seem to be not so intimidated by history as their elders. The elders lived it. Across the spectrum of racial and ethnic groups in this country, because of the absence of those extremely negative experiences, it is difficult for young people of all persuasions to comprehend that such a history is real. The disbelief is genuine and is both positive and negative in terms of grounds to protect the future from repeating itself. Disbelief is positive in that it reflects young people's view of an idealistic society. They view society as it should be, not as it is. But that is where the impetus for correction resides. The disbelief is negative in that it is likely to produce denial, which results in complacency and inactivity.

The cleavage between the two men ran deep. But there was also a measure of mutual respect, for both felt that the intent of the other was genuine concern for the well-being of the race. Du Bois had appreciation for Washington as an intellectual, but was critical of how that intellect was used. He appreciated his rival's efforts to elevate the status of African Americans and was reluctant to criticize all but his methodology.

Du Bois' own education was accomplished by working his way through college, saving summer earnings for tuition. He earned a bachelor's degree at Fisk University and was the first African American to earn a doctorate at Harvard University. He did studies at the University of Berlin, taught Greek and Latin at Wilberforce University, and taught sociology at Atlanta University. His background reveals the extraordinary value he placed on education. Because of what he observed in society he was not deluded into thinking that acquiring an education was a cure-all. But education afforded one a better promise of worthy pursuits and a self-concept that industrial occupations alone could not provide. Washington's approach would offer only the promise of the status quo, which was not acceptable. Advancement would require knowledge. Knowledge would be required to appreciate the need to vote. Intelligent voting would require both formal and informal education. In spite of his respect for Washington, the debate between them never ceased during their lifetimes. And though the issue is not as controversial today, it should continue to be debated, for not to do so may allow mediocrity to resurface without discussion.

As early as 1837 it was recognized that provisions for Blacks to be educated were nonexistent. Efforts to ameliorate the situation would be left up to Blacks themselves with few resources. In line with Du Bois' platform, much of the urgency, though not all, was placed on higher education for Black men, a situation which was to change with the passage of two and a half decades, when Spelman College, the first college for Black women, was founded (the author's mother was an alumna.) The significance of education (especially higher education) is expressed by the special efforts exerted by African American churches in establishing institutions of higher learning, as evidenced by the African Methodist Episcopal Church's founding of Wilberforce University in 1856 and Meharry Medical College in 1876. The African American church has historically found itself in the forefront of social movements in the interest of promoting Black causes, including the civil rights movement.

Other noteworthy milestones included The Tuskegee Normal and Industrial Institute in Alabama, founded by Booker T. Washington. Though it sounded and looked suspiciously like Washington's "racial uplift" with his emphasis on practical application of knowledge, it was also considered "higher learning" at the time. Other milestones involved the inevitable conflict that comes with demands made on the establishment for changes in social institutions, especially regarding education, which was seen as the keystone to social change. Conflicts involved integration of Central High School in Little Rock, Arkansas in 1957, (note that the "Little Rock Nine" was comprised of seven women and three men, the seventh woman was Daisy Bates, president of the Arkansas branch of the NAACP); the notorious incident of James Meredith being escorted to enroll at the University of Mississippi in 1962, and Alabama Governor George Wallace blocking the doorway of the University of Alabama to prevent the enrollment of two African American students. The changes that have occurred have not come about without trauma, but the anguish suffered by those who pursued the evolving results would willingly make the necessary expected sacrifices.

African Americans have focused massive attention on higher education. This extended "reach" is called for because of the potential to influence decision-making by occupying important positions in society. Access to institutions of higher learning has been sporadic at best. Therein lay the necessity for Blacks to find alternative routes to attain college training. Traditionally Black colleges did not occur to promote racial separation. They developed because they were denied admission to established White colleges and universities. Although this denial was based on premeditated and indefensible results, the consequences proved to present relatively positive outcomes. For example, one of the several favorable outcomes was the development of the Historically Black Colleges and Universities, (HBCUs) in Southwest Atlanta, Georgia, which produced the Atlanta University Center Consortium, Inc., consisting of Clark Atlanta University, Spelman College (a woman's college), Morehouse College (a men's college), and Morehouse School of Medicine. The Consortium allows students to cross-register for a broader educational experience and shares the Robert W. Woodruff Library. This impressive collaboration of institutions developed out of rejection and necessity. Other historically Black colleges and universities have existed for the same reasons. Rejection can sometimes result in creativity and self-sufficiency.

LATINO AND HISPANIC AMERICANS

Richard Rodriguez, literature professor and essayist, was born to working–class Mexican immigrants (Henslin 80). He had a difficult time making adjustments to English-speaking schools. His experience is not unique among Latino Americans. It addresses the issue of a native language's worth, but goes deeper in doing a poor job of dealing with cultural differences. The debate persists about the obligation of immigrants to acquire English skills as a prerequisite to become a full-fledged citizen, or at the least to participate in society equally as a non-citizen. The absence of competence in English puts one at a striking disadvantage in American society. It is an issue that must be put in context, however. While it becomes necessary to acquire such skills, it should not be required to divest one of his or her native tongue in the process. One's language is inevitably related to one's culture. To dismiss one is to dismiss the other. It is this circumstance that elevates the value of bilingualism to an exemplary state.

It is important to clarify the difference between Hispanics and Latinos, and even Afro-Latinos. The terms are not interchangeable, although they are often treated as such. The two terms are indeed confusing, even to those who identify themselves as one or the other. The term "Hispanic" is said to refer primarily to language. "Latino," on the other hand, relates to geography and has virtually displaced the term "Chicano." Hispanic is most often used on the Eastern Seaboard for people coming from countries speaking Spanish. "Latino" is most likely to be used west of the Mississippi, typically referring to people from the Caribbean (Puerto Rico, Cuba, the Dominican Republic) and South and Central America. The majority of Mexican Americans reside in the American Southwest. In recent times, however, many are opting for regions throughout the country. As a Southern African American, it is sometimes really difficult to fathom Mexican Americans and Asian Americans settling in my childhood hometown. For the most part during that childhood, only Blacks and Whites lived there. A good guess is that the diffusion of other groups into the region has to do with economic opportunities. In the past, practically all immigrants from Mexico settled in California (especially Southern

California) and Texas. Migration patterns reflect what is called the "push-pull" imperative. Human beings leave places that are not functional for them and move to areas that show more promise. Imagine a Honda plant in Alabama that attracts workers from without. Or Hyundai plants in Alabama and Georgia with the same results. Corporations also move from place to place for economic reasons.

Taking a further look at Richard Rodriguez's experiences, one sees the implications of emersion in language and, therefore, cultural skills at an early stage in educational development. Experiences in the home, regardless of race or ethnicity, are extremely likely to influence potential for future educational success. Family's attitudes about language and culture are as diverse as families themselves. Some parents absolutely insist that their children divest themselves of their native tongues in the attempt to promote the possibility of career and, therefore, economic success. In fact, only English may be permitted in the home. Others may choose to communicate exclusively in the language of their country of origin in the home. This may prove to be a lackluster effort to enhance cultural solidarity and preservation. Or in some cases it has to do with the inability or unwillingness of parents to acquire English skills themselves, causing the unlikelihood of children having the opportunity to communicate in English routinely in the home setting. It is commonly known that the later in life one attempts to learn a new language, the more difficult it is likely to be. As mentioned previously, when groups choose to join new cultures, it is incumbent upon them to acquire the cultural norms of the new group. That means the especially important factor of language. The potential for future prosperity depends on it.

Educational systems do not always consider the need to accommodate the gap between where students are and where they need to be in order to accomplish society's demands. And too often the students are held responsible for their shortcomings. What is forgotten in the process is the responsibility of education. Unfortunately, in our society there is no room for diversity in the educational process. One standard must fit all. That is very difficult in a society as diverse as ours. Even among native speakers there is no room for individual backgrounds and capabilities. The "one-size-fits-all" syndrome is the dominant principal upon which all outcomes rest. This is a major barrier for all groups in society, but a double-whammy for those who must first overcome cultural differences and then meet the requirements of conventional academic programs. The programs are typically unforgiving, and it becomes simply a matter of sink-or-swim for those who are not properly prepared. Educational systems cannot be considered to be successful if they do not provide the enlightenment by which they are defined. The "one-size-fits-all" concept is a blight on the American educational system. It is not an ill-conceived principle applied exclusively to the underclass in America, but to all who would avail themselves of public education opportunities.

Our system was born from noble beginnings. In the effort to ensure that this relatively new nation developed a uniform national culture, Thomas Jefferson and Noah Webster proposed universal schooling, using standardized texts (Henslin 476). Context is crucial here, for as dissimilar as the population was at that time, it would become more so as the decades passed. Our society continues to learn how difficult it is to develop a uniform national culture from a very diverse population. It would seem that the first order of business would be to develop a level of consensus as to what are the core values in the society. Education is defined as one of the more essential core values, perhaps because so many other elements are contingent upon it. Complications arise because very often minority groups are apt to "circle-the-wagons" as a defensive strategy. This often develops subcultures and countercultures with their own interpretation of what is important. This does not serve the concept of uniformity very well and may, in fact, cause dissension. The likelihood that some groups may see the importance of education differently is a real probability. A number of factors may contribute to this assessment by a group. One factor may be the social distance between the teacher and the student. This often produces distrust and suspicion in both directions, which is likely to lessen the potential for effective teacher-learner collaboration. Teachers should have had some intervention, which is likely to decrease the likelihood of such conflict. On the other hand, there is a good chance that most learners have probably had no such preparation for this new venture. The preparation may come after the fact, which slows down the learning process.

The notion of uniformity presents many issues in society in general, and in education in particular. How does the educational institution meld cultural differences and the desire for uniform outcomes for all students, regardless of backgrounds? This is obviously a difficult task that has been undertaken with zeal in many settings. It is also a task that is constantly under question in some quarters. Our education system is either incapable or unwilling to treat individual idiosyncrasies as unique, so why should anyone expect it to place high emphasis on group differences? In reaction to the massive size and complexity of the society, the accent is placed on getting as many students through the system uniformly as possible. In a program that I oversaw as an administrator, we used a program of Individualized Education Plans (IEPs) that were designed to respond to the unique requirements of each student. Each program followed each student throughout her or his journey in the program.

I have on occasion questioned why such an approach is not offered to all students, as opposed to only those with special needs. Basic learning theory teaches us that all students do not learn the same way. Some learn best by tactile experiences, some by reading and following instructions, and some best by emulating others. The usual response to my query revolves around cost, that we cannot afford to address each student's needs. The cost would be prohibitive. Well-reasoned thinking would indicate that we cannot afford *not* to respond to individual needs. With students, we are dealing with our important human resources. The cost of IEPs would not begin to compare with other expenditures, such as space exploration, defense spending, and financial support for foreign governments. While these outlays can be defended as important to our national security, there is something to be said for prioritization for the nation's future. By failing to consider individual and group differences, a major segment of the society will continue to be left floundering in ignorance.

More serious attention needs to be given the impact of de facto segregation on life chances of groups living in poverty. Hispanics and blacks living in poverty areas in inner cities are likely to be burdened with reduced opportunities for economic advancement due to fewer productive career options. Those options are directly related to where education has taken them (or not taken them). We live in what has been defined as a credential society, where job opportunities are most often tied to degrees and diplomas. Degrees and diplomas are disproportionately distributed among social class groups. The biggest obstacle for Latinos in the job market is the absence of English language skills. Without access to meaningful educational opportunities, chances of competing in the job market are virtually non-existent. And so it goes: education has an impact on job opportunities; job opportunities have an impact on earning capacity; earning capacity has an impact on housing and residential areas; residential areas have an impact on education, which is affected by community schools and potential for higher education. It all begins and ends with education. So, to be left out of that cycle means to be left out of society's rewards. Too often, Latinos have been seen simply as cheap labor, which requires no academic skills. Others may see them as such, but with growing awareness, they see themselves in a different light as major participants in society's valued enterprises.

The United States expresses strong preference for immigrants entering the country to have a grasp of English, or to be on the path to acquiring proficiency. The requirement is a positive one, since not to have the ability to speak the language is almost guaranteed to result in failure. Ironically, Americans seem to be the least willing to learn the languages of other cultures, even when visiting host countries. Ethnocentrism tells us that the culture is unworthy. Therefore, the language is unworthy. Globalism and multiculturalism are making that attitude increasingly problematic for any country that clings to provincialism. We live in an interdependent world, which demands that none is totally self-sufficient. The skills that immigrants lack require that the "inclusive" education system have provisions to bring them up to speed. Attempts to do just that are in place, but not without detractors. The enduring question is the following: Do we make special contingencies for those without the skills? Ample resistance to do anything other than work within the system already established also persists. This is where the problem is often exacerbated, for those who do seem to keep pace are then marginalized, which sets in motion a downward spiral to defeatism. The path forward offers nothing less than self-condemnation. Failure builds upon failure.

Hispanics are over-represented among the poor for several reasons. Immigrants start out at a disadvantage due to the language barrier, but also due to stereotypes and prejudices, which subject them to unflattering expectations. Consider, for example, the image of the lazy Mexican, sitting against a cactus plant, wearing a serape and a sombrero pulled down over his eyes. Real experience tells us that this is anything but the truth.

One has but to witness work crews in the neighborhood to appreciate what is industriousness, men running from point A to point B continuously from morning to dusk or the men gathered in front of Home Depot or donut stores with brown lunch bags seeking to work for an honest dollar. Notice how early the streets are crowded with men on bicycles, and strawberry fields are filled with seas of human beings with their backs bent, potentially for the full day. I always think, "These are not lazy people." A representative number of people sitting in corporate executive offices and in cubicles could be better defined as lazy. The examples given here are of people some distance from receiving the benefits necessary to ascend to favorable statuses in American society. But the group as a whole is making gigantic strides towards full participation.

ASIAN AMERICANS

The tendency among many in our society is to categorize all people of Asian descent into a single racial and ethnic group. Before proceeding with a discussion of Asian Americans, it is necessary to clarify how the groups should be perceived. The perceptions should be based on the history of each ethnicity—how and why it arrived in the United States, what happened to it in the aftermath of its arrival, and what its status is today. The long list of Asian Americans includes, in alphabetical order, Bangladeshi and Pakistani, Cambodian, Chinese, Filipino, Hmong, Indian, Japanese, Korean, Laotian, Native Hawaiian and Pacific Islander, Taiwanese, and Vietnamese. The largest Asian American groups are:

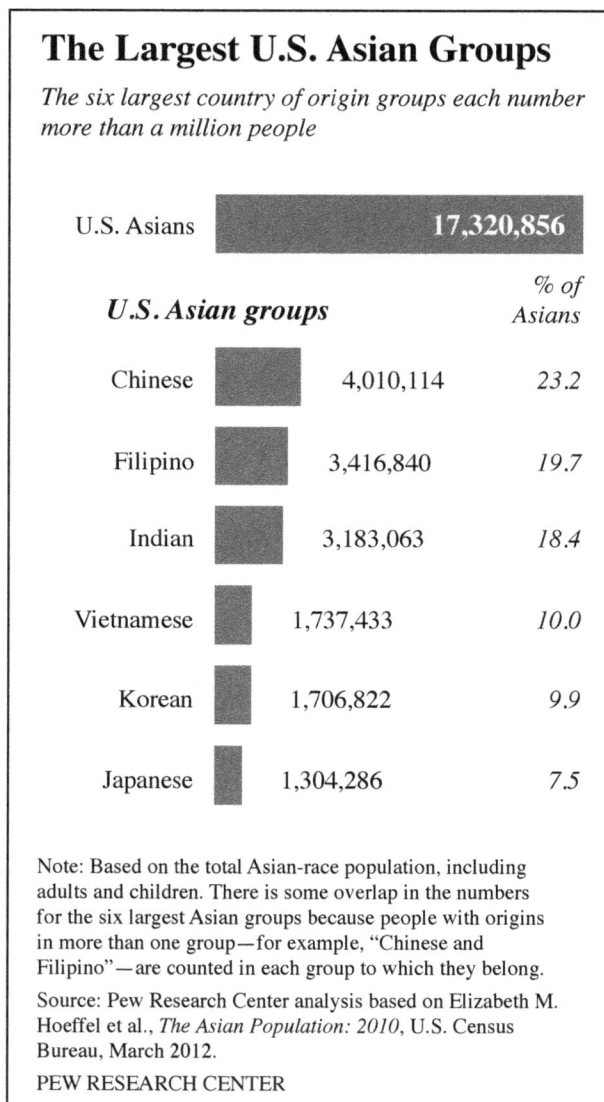

The Largest U.S. Asian Groups

The six largest country of origin groups each number more than a million people

U.S. Asian groups		% of Asians
U.S. Asians	17,320,856	
Chinese	4,010,114	23.2
Filipino	3,416,840	19.7
Indian	3,183,063	18.4
Vietnamese	1,737,433	10.0
Korean	1,706,822	9.9
Japanese	1,304,286	7.5

Note: Based on the total Asian-race population, including adults and children. There is some overlap in the numbers for the six largest Asian groups because people with origins in more than one group—for example, "Chinese and Filipino"—are counted in each group to which they belong.

Source: Pew Research Center analysis based on Elizabeth M. Hoeffel et al., *The Asian Population: 2010*, U.S. Census Bureau, March 2012.

PEW RESEARCH CENTER

Some of these groups maintain higher profiles than others in contemporary society. The history of each is longer than is typically imagined. And each history is marked with sordid treatment by American hosts. Each group was influenced by the previcusly mentioned "push-pull" factors. Many came with the intention of returning home with untold riches. Some were conscripted for the enhancement of their hosts' riches. But, unlike the Africans, none were brought over in chains. Conditions were such that they might as well have been. The higher profile ones, the ones that are most often discussed in our society today are the Japanese Americans, the Chinese Americans, the Vietnamese Americans, and the Korean Americans. At issue here is the impact of education on each of these groups. At issue here is the impact of education on each of these groups. Please note below that the Chinese are ranked third among U. S. Asian groups in Bachelor degrees and above. Also, Asian Americans, as a group, lead others in education and income:

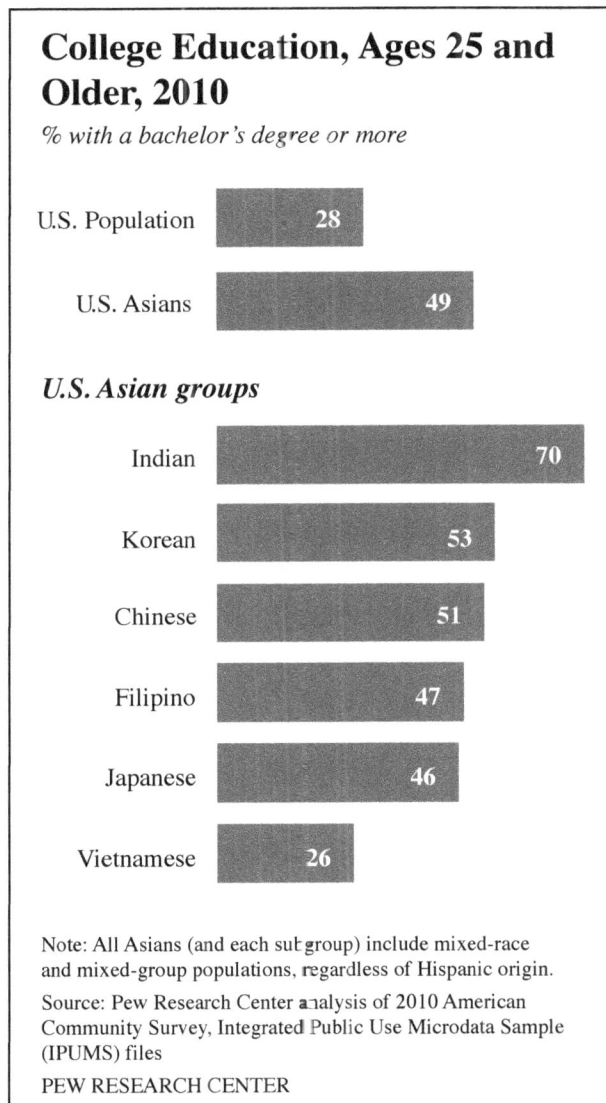

College Education, Ages 25 and Older, 2010

% with a bachelor's degree or more

U.S. Population — 28

U.S. Asians — 49

U.S. Asian groups

Indian — 70

Korean — 53

Chinese — 51

Filipino — 47

Japanese — 46

Vietnamese — 26

Note: All Asians (and each subgroup) include mixed-race and mixed-group populations, regardless of Hispanic origin.

Source: Pew Research Center analysis of 2010 American Community Survey, Integrated Public Use Microdata Sample (IPUMS) files

PEW RESEARCH CENTER

From "Rise of Asian Americans" by Pew Research Center - Social & Demographic Trends. Copyright © 2012 by Pew Research Center. Reprinted by permission.

Asian Americans Lead Others In Education, Income

% with a bachelor's degree or more, among ages 25 and older, 2010

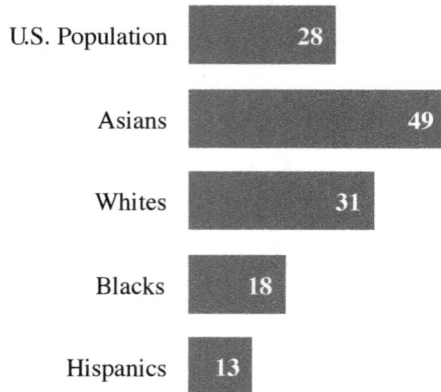

U.S. Population	28
Asians	49
Whites	31
Blacks	18
Hispanics	13

Median household income, 2010

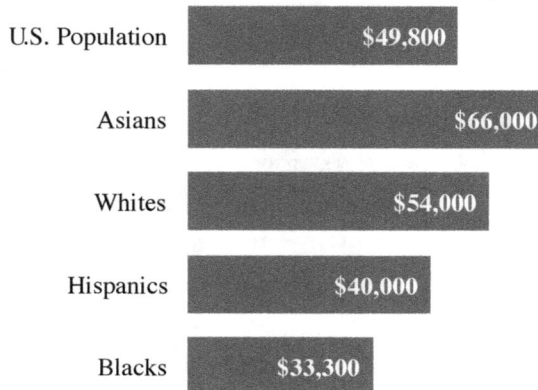

U.S. Population	$49,800
Asians	$66,000
Whites	$54,000
Hispanics	$40,000
Blacks	$33,300

Note: Asians include mixed-race Asian population, regardless of Hispanic origin. Whites and blacks include only non-Hispanics. Hispanics are of any race. Household income is based on householders ages 18 and older; race and ethnicity are based on those of household head.

Source: Pew Research Center analysis of 2010 American Community Survey, Integrated Public Use Microdata Sample (IPUMS) files

Japanese Americans

Following is a partial vignette on the experiences of Harry H.L. Kitano (1926–2002), Professor of Social Welfare and Sociology and Acting Director of the Asian American Study Center at UCLA.

> *I grew up in San Francisco surrounded by a variety of different ethnic groups. My parents were from Japan, but I lived in Chinatown, which was close to the Italian section. So I had acquaintances from a variety of backgrounds. Names that I can remember from early school days were Padillo, Derrivan, Wong, Francesconi, and Lee. I remember how we jeered a new student from France*

named Donat—he came to school in a shirt, tie, and knickers and therefore warranted the name of "frog." We practiced prejudice and discrimination, but we were totally unfamiliar with these terms. Being Japanese in the middle of Chinatown certainly made for differences. There was an elementary school right across the street from where I lived, but it was for "Chinese students" only.

. . . The first time I remember hearing the term sociology was in a World War II concentration camp for people of Japanese ancestry. It should be recalled that after the Japanese attack on Pearl Harbor in 1941, all people of Japanese ancestry residing along the West Coast, whether citizens or not, were sent to "relocation camps" scattered throughout the United States. I was a high school student at the time, and during one of our endless discussions concerning our internment, I remember one fellow saying that a "sociological perspective" would give us insight into why we were imprisoned in such camps. My guess is that none of us knew what that meant, but we all nodded wisely and agreed.Farley 322–323).

At the very mention of Japanese Americans and the level of discrimination they have endured, the immediate thought goes to World War Two and the internment camps, to which they were sent for the duration of the war. This is not the worst thing that has happened to racial or ethnic groups in the U. S., but it is certainly near the top of the list. This was a direct affront to the very principle of equal treatment to all citizens, regardless of race, creed, or previous conditions of servitude. Their history needs to be reviewed in light of where they were prior to the war in terms of education attainment, economic standing, and social perceptions. In other words, what did they lose as the result of their internment? It is difficult for many in our society to comprehend, first, how they coped with their situation, and, second, how they recovered, seemingly without malice. Was it a generational issue? Did the older generation tend to be more passive and accepting of their plight? Prior to being sent off to the internment camps, (which some would define as concentration camps), they were dispossessed of all that they owned, including their homes, businesses, farms, currency and anything else of value. Descriptions of those camps, such as the Manzanar Relocation Center in California, are horrifying, cramming a total family into one room and restricting normal family activity. In many cases gender was not observed, and women were in quarters with men who were not their husbands. Of the 120,000 people who were interned, 80,000 were American citizens. Was this treatment a racial issue? We were at war with Germany and Italy as well, and neither was rounded up and put into internment camps. One explanation for this unequal treatment revolves around the physical distinction between German and Italian Americans verses Japanese Americans. The Japanese Americans were said to be easily identifiable. But this conclusion was flawed as well, for often distinctions are not made among the various Asian groups because of similar physical characteristics. After all, don't they all look alike?

Another plausible explanation for singling out the Japanese Americans might be that German Americans constitute the largest White American ethnic group in the United States. Rounding them or Italian Americans up would leave fewer white Americans in the population. Another logistical explanation was the perceived threat of Japanese espionage on the West Coast where most Japanese Americans resided. None of the explanations made the outcome justifiable. 113 Eventually congress concluded that the internment had not been justified and many years later decided that restitution was in order and awarded some of the surviving internees $20,000 each. Twenty thousand was not nearly enough to make up for their losses in the early forties and, due to inflation, was worth much less after several decades. The restitution was a pittance in today's money. Many consumers have credit card limits of twenty thousand dollars today. This was hardly just compensation for all they had lost. In addition, after such a long period, many of them were no longer alive. Several U.S. presidents have offered apologies for what has been recognized as a mistake, including not only George W. Bush, but also Ronald Reagan and Bill Clinton. Bush signed the Civil Rights Act of 1988 (HR442), awarding redress to all surviving internees or their relatives. Bush sent a formal apology along with a check for $20,000. To admit that the internment was a mistake is obviously the proper thing to do. But one has to wonder about the extent of the damage done and if history can repeat itself. Following is George W. Bush's letter of apology to the internees:

A monetary sum and words alone cannot restore lost years or erase painful memories; neither can they fully convey our Nation's resolve to rectify injustice and to uphold the rights of individuals. We can never fully right the wrongs of the past. But we can take a clear stand for justice and recognize that serious injustices were done to Japanese Americans during World War II.

In enacting a law calling for restitution and offering a sincere apology, your fellow Americans have, in a very real sense, renewed their traditional commitment to the ideals of freedom, equality, and justice. You and your family have our best wishes for the future.

Sincerely,

[signature: G. Bush]

Important questions about the internment of the Japanese Americans relate to the educational process for their children while incarcerated. What was that experience? And what impact would the experience have on the future of education for Japanese Americans? Is there a correlation between the harsh treatment and the group's extraordinary academic achievements today? One would hope not. For to accept that premise would indicate that hardships and mistreatments are prerequisites for future success. This idea is the very personification and classic definition of the slippery slope fallacy. It is dangerous to assume that it is acceptable to denigrate human beings in the interest of facilitating a better future for them. History has shown us that denigration most often inflicts such damage on people that recovery is highly unlikely. The experience of education and Japanese Americans is interesting in that few other groups have suffered the same indignities and recovered as well, including other Asian Americans. Society needs to debunk the notion that "hard times are good for you." The notion only works if people survive the ordeal. For example, in the example of African Americans, recovery is still a work in progress after arrival in Jamestown in 1619. Hard times have been experienced by all Asian Americans, but most would argue that the Japanese nightmare stands out as the most shameful.

As early as 1906, the law segregated Whites and Asians in schools (modeled after the Jim Crow laws in the South.) Education has been of prime importance to Japanese Americans before, during, and after the internment debacle. Evidence of the emphasis on schooling during the incarceration is reflected in the interns' negotiation for nearly autonomous establishment of educational opportunities for their children. This was apparently a traditional value established pre-internment, which was carried on during incarceration. The relative level of educational autonomy was permitted, in spite of debilitating restrictions in practically all other areas. This worked well towards perpetuating an age-old value that would prove to be one that often defines the group. In the United States today, Japanese Americans are said to be the most educated and literate population in the modern world. The curriculum in Japanese schools is very demanding by U. S. standards and requires student commitment beyond that which is required in most U. S. schools (Bryjak and Soroka 134).

The culture is carried over in the immigration process. That culture emphasizes the importance of education as an instrument to promote not only group well-being, but national vitality as well. The concept of the pre-eminence of the group over the individual runs counter to the U. S. emphasis on individuality. Individualism encourages a level of competition. And while that competition has been credited with the growth and vitality of our capitalistic society, it has come at a price. It reminds us of Herbert Spencer's notion of "survival of the fittest." There will continue to be debate as to which is most functional for society– the concerns of the few or the concerns of the many. The "group consensus" philosophy of the Japanese has worked very well for them on a rather communal level. Traditionally, there was no provision for individual advancement at the expense of the masses. The education system in Japan revolves around that philosophy, which is thought by many to be explanation for its success. That concept, with some degree of variation, manifests itself among many Japanese Americans over the several generations as learners in all levels of the American education system. To argue that one system is superior to the other would best be based on the outcomes. Even so, the conclusions are likely to be subjective, again, being based upon societal orientation.

The American education system is fertile ground for scholars with the Japanese orientation towards matriculation through the system. Success is measured by achieving lofty grades. Such achievement is often accomplished via rote memory. Often concepts take second place to the ability to regurgitate and critically evaluate what has been said or read. Group collaboration in settings, such as study groups, enhances the potential for success for all involved. Performance on exams is usually high; however, discussion of concepts tends to go lacking. Certainly, cultural emphasis on educational achievement and family insistence on hard work and positive results play important roles in the overall success rate of education for Japanese Americans. The values are so embedded that it should be no surprise that what was a cultural imperative in Japan before World War Two, in the U.S. prior to the incarceration and during incarceration, would be sustained in the aftermath of the war. Whatever conclusion one draws about the value of emphasis on group integrity over individualism and the value of education, a definite correlation seems to exist between educational success and economic viability.

That the interned Japanese Americans managed to maintain their focus on education under the direst of circumstances is nothing short of incredible. Granted, they were permitted to organize and administer their own schooling in the camps, but only in exchange for ensuring that the proper indoctrination was included in the curriculum. That indoctrination was designed to prepare the internees for their proper Americanized role post-internment. They were required to learn about democracy, which many were already indoctrinated to because they were American citizens, even as they were confined behind barbed-wire fences. Another inconsistency was the enlistment in the U.S. Army of Japanese American soldiers, who comprised the 442nd Regimental Combat Team and were fighting in Europe as their families were relocated into the camps. They were the most decorated infantry regiment in U.S. Army history. As with the internees, the wonder is how that sort of loyalty could be sustained under those conditions. Was it because they had no other choice, or was it an opportunity to prove the point that they were worthy American citizens? How much of the level of acceptance had to do with the historical emphasis of Japanese education in pre-modern and postwar times?

The positive image that is typically applied to middle- and upper-class Asians assigns a label to them that is anything but positive. The notion of "the model minority" is recognized as a myth, since regardless of the group's social status, they are often depicted as pliable, intelligent, passive, and exceptionally patient and industrious. Obviously, all of these descriptors cannot be applied to all Asian Americans. Many of the Asian Americans' value systems do, indeed, resemble those of the White majority. A consequence of this is a higher level of acceptance on the part of Whites. "They're kind of like us." During the chaotic times of riots and demonstrations in the 50's and 60's, this was a group that was not about to be involved in disrespectful and disorderly activities. The patience that they exhibited stood them in good stead with the majority. The "model minority" concept is a myth because, in spite of their successes, they still encounter prejudice and discrimination. Passivity and patience is not highly valued in this competitive society. The model American tag certainly has not worked for Asian Americans when it comes to admissions in many American universities. Beginning in the 1980's, many universities became concerned with what was believed to be inordinate numbers of Asians enrolling, discordant with their actual percentage in the general population. It was especially problematic at some of the University of California campuses, where Asian Americans felt that they were being discriminated against because of their relative high numbers. It has become increasingly difficult to sell the "model minority" concept to many of the younger generations of Asian Americans. Many of them still resentment among them regarding the way their ancestors were treated during WWII.

Relative to the restructuring of education in post-war Japan, Ronald Anderson writes:

> Over the years, Japan has revamped her education system a number of times. With the coming of the U. S. Education Mission in 1946, she turned her schools towards democratization. The major aims of this reform program in education were: 1) the elimination of militarism and ultranationalism; 2) democratization; 3) modernization; and 4) decentralization of education control. Specific reforms included: 1) the provision of greater equality of educational opportunity through the conversion of the multiple-track into a single-track system; 2) an additional three years of compulsory education; 3) coeducation at all levels; and, 4) general education at the secondary and higher levels. To train intelligent participation in a democracy, a new content was introduced – notably social studies at the elementary and secondary levels. During the present period, some of these goals and reforms have been modified, however, the essential goals remain: suiting education to life, helping the individual to develop his ability, and the goal of freedom of speech and action. ("Japan")

Japanese culture, and by extension education, is based on Buddhism and Confusion principles, which stress literary skills, the classics, and learning. These values have been perpetuated through the centuries and manifest themselves in the way Japanese education is perceived today. When the education of Japanese American children is discussed among other Americans, one of the first reasons given for their success is the family tradition, which requires hard work and academic success. It seems that competition has not been deemphasized, as one might think, for the measurement of success is based upon how one does compared to others. In fact, as some Americans see the need for their system to emulate the Japanese, others find the Japanese system to be flawed for it discourages the competition, which is felt by some to be the basis of American enterprise. In the meantime, there is a bit of de-emphasis of the group consensus model in Japan as it borrows methods from other systems that tend to be successful, especially economically. Both the Japanese and American models have moved towards a form of hybridization, borrowing elements of cultural approaches from each. This is a direct consequence of globalization. That hybridization has great influence on what makes many Japanese American children the way they are today. There continues to be cultural borrowing in both directions as each culture attempts to enhance its status. The lending and borrowing of cultural ways among cultures, in the parlance of anthropologists, is called cultural diffusion.

Chinese Americans

The so-called "yellow peril" stereotype involved both the Japanese Americans and Chinese Americans. It is yet another instance of racism, which, when viewed in retrospect, is based on fear and unsubstantiated belief that Asians proposed to dominate world culture. While negative attitudes towards Japanese Americans were based upon wartime antagonism, attitudes towards Chinese Americans were base, primarily, on a tide of emigration, which threatened to erode the influence of established American culture. In reality, consideration should be given to the effects of a two-way transformation, for as Asian Americans become more and more "Americanized," they tend to lose some of their native culture. In the meantime, Americans are fascinated with the success rates of Asian Americans, both academically and economically, and constantly compare and contrast educational methods of both groups. The emphasis is, probably for good reason, on outcomes. Ever since the Russians deployed Sputnik, the first venture into space exploration, the world has been preoccupied with math and the sciences, which are seen as the basis for success. Japanese education tends to excel in these two areas. Because Asians are often lumped together as a single group, what is seen to be characteristic of one group spills over into other groups that look alike physically. Some will benefit from the positive reputations of other Asian Americans. By the same token, some will be categorized negatively along with other groups that are not viewed in a positive light.

According to the U.S. Census Bureau, Chinese Americans are the largest Asian American group (See table on page 49). The first of what was seen as an incursion of large numbers of Chinese nationals into the United States occurred in the mid-1800s. Almost any discussion of the introduction of Chinese to the United States begins with the subjects of "Chinese Coolies." Sordid accounts of how they were treated abound. Theirs is yet another example of how most immigrants have been greeted as they sought better living conditions for themselves and their families by coming to the "land of opportunity." California was the destination of choice because of the promise of gold and work on the railroads. Little did they know what awaited them, especially after the construction of the railroads was completed. The surplus of workers was seen as a threat to American workers and their jobs. The "pull" that brought them to these shores in the first place now reverted to the "push" that invited them to leave, which was not easy to accomplish. This situation is analogous to the contemporary predicament of many farm workers from Mexico today who have found that conditions of the U.S. economy have evolved negatively, so that the situation south of the border may be more inviting.

Attitudes towards the Chinese immigrants provoked passage of the Chinese Exclusion Act of 1882. No other specific immigrant group has been subjected to exclusionary policies to the extent of those affecting the Chinese. Inroads to the United States were cut off sharply. The two primary reasons that there was such resentment towards the Chinese immigrant were (1) they were willing to work for very low wages, undercutting American workers and (2) people thought that too much gold was being sent back to China, wealth that should be retained in the U. S. for its own economic vitality.

The Chinese Exclusion Repeal Act was enacted sixty-five years later in 1943, when China became an ally to the U.S. during World War II. Chinese Americans became actively involved in the war effort on America's behalf during that campaign. That involvement, along with collaboration with China as an ally, made it difficult to establish and maintain immigration laws that were discriminatory against Chinese immigration. It is interesting that such consideration would be in order at that point in light of the blatant, unreasoned, and unjustifiable discrimination involving Japanese Americans in the 1940s. So, as Japanese Americans were being herded into concentration camps, the Chinese Exclusion Repeal Act opened the doors in the 1960s for increased numbers of Chinese immigrants who tended to be more educated and economically stable than their predecessors. It seems that the later the immigration, the more acceptable the immigrants. But there are other considerations as well. What is the value of the immigrant to the United States? This has always been a determining factor in setting immigration allowances. What are the needs of the country? The United States did not need the Chinese in 1882 and later, for there was the threat of the "yellow peril." There was a glut of Chinese immigrants and a shortage of jobs. During World War II, the U.S. needed every able-bodied person available to assist in the war effort. Remember "Rosie the Riveter"? In addition, China became an ally of the United States during World War II, perhaps for strategic reasons. Nevertheless, that alliance improved the situation for Chinese Americans, again for strategic reasons.

The more recent immigrants entered the country with not only more education, but also more work skills. Another example of the United States' willingness to take in immigrants on the basis of national need is the use of scientists from enemy countries, such as Germany, during World War II. This could be justified because after all, we are a nation of immigrants, and we use whatever resources are available to us for our purposes. Though often these policies seem unfair, other countries use the same prescription. The difference is that the United States accepts more immigrants than all other nations combined. In spite of the discrimination, the United States seems to be the destination of choice.

Like all other groups that immigrate to the United States, the Chinese, while too often characterized as simply overachievers and academically superior, come in a variety of social statuses. Like all other Americans, they reside in a variety of communities, based on such things as affordability and/or de facto segregation. A consequence of residential circumstance is most often related to educational opportunity. In the classroom setting they are typically prone to excel on exams, leaving their classmates in the dust. But there are also those who barely get by, in spite of their efforts, and those who do not meet minimum standards. Sometimes this is the result of a family background that does not provide requisite motivation and resources, and, like all other groups, the problem may reflect the individual's native ability. In any case, such instances substantially debunk the concept of the "model minority." Too often our society makes assumptions about the many groups that comprise us on preconceived notions based on unsubstantiated stereotypes. For Asian Americans in general this is both a curse and a blessing. It becomes a curse when one is incapable of living up to society's expectations and a blessing when one is assumed capable of meeting the expectations so that the outcome becomes a foregone conclusion. It amounts to a wonderful kind of pressure. Very often one is simply given the benefit of the doubt. This educator has witnessed unbearable amounts of frustration on the part of Asian American students who cannot meet the educational institution's requirements, but also their family's expectations.

Of the four million Chinese Americans who reside in the United States, the majority live in urban areas, such as California, (primarily in San Francisco), New York, Texas, and Hawaii. In spite of humble beginnings, Chinese Americans are generally doing well educationally and economically today. Median income for single-race Asian Americans is $68,780 (Kendall 264). Some, however, have not escaped their humble beginnings and find themselves stuck in menial occupations, which translate to menial pay, housing, political positions, and most importantly, educational opportunities. It is interesting that as with other minority groups, the image that is conjured in the minds of other Americans is the image of the downtrodden. Assessments and opinions are made on the basis of the least affluent of the group. One has but to dig a little more deeply to conclude that the situation of this stratum is not only a complete picture of the group, but also ignores the valuable contributions of immigrants who are achievers and who abide by society's rules of engagement. To ignore these achievements is to disparage some of our most revered values. Chinese Americans have experienced high levels of success as professionals, business entrepreneurs, and technical experts (Kendall 264). Chinese Americans have made substantial political gains throughout the United States, but especially in San Francisco where they occupy key positions in municipal government and in the education system. Ironically, this evolution all started with the introduction of the "coolies" who worked the railroads in Northern California. Although most Chinese workers were employed in lower tiered occupations in 1870, their household incomes were higher than the U.S. average at $49,800.00, and almost equal to the U. S. Asian average at $66,000.00. See chart below:

Household Income, 2010

Median

U.S. Population	$49,800
U.S. Asians	$66,000

U.S. Asian groups

Indian	$88,000
Filipino	$75,000
Japanese	$65,390
Chinese	$65,050
Vietnamese	$53,400
Korean	$50,000

Note: Based on householders ages 18 and older. Race and Asian subgroup based on those of household head. All Asians (and each subgroup) include mixed-race and mixed-group populations, regardless of Hispanic origin.

Source: Pew Research Center analysis of 2010 American Community Survey, Integrated Public Use Microdata Sample (IPUMS) files

PEW RESEARCH CENTER

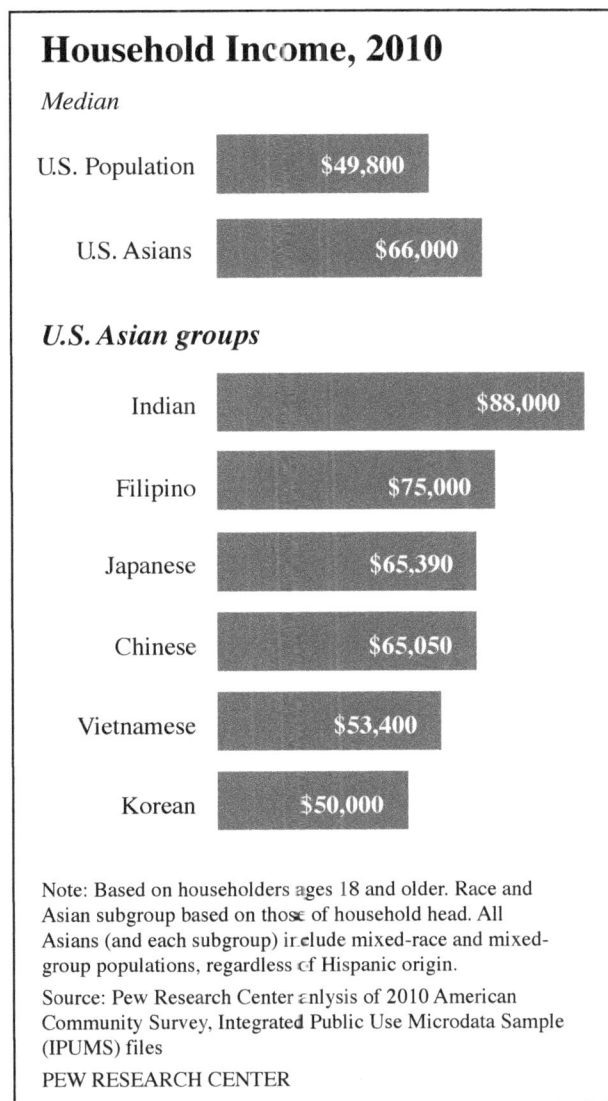

Because of the historical antagonism in Asia among the various Asian nations, some remnants of those experiences have been present in the United States. Much of the animosity seems to have subsided in recent times as political awareness has taken hold and groups have collaborated in efforts to enhance the quality of life for all. A number of Asian American organizations that recognize problems common to the entire group have emerged. Some of the more prominent ones are:

Asian American Bar Association

Asian American Journalists Association

Asian Community Mental Health Services

Asian Law Caucus

Asian Professional Exchange

Asian Business Association

Asian Pacific Women's Center

Asian American Government Executives Network

Asian Family & Community Empowerment Center

Asian American Youth Alliance

Asian American Institute

Asian American Political Association

Some notable political leaders have been Senator Daniel Inouye of Hawaii, U.S. Assistant Attorney General for Civil Rights Bill Lann Lee, Governor Gary Locke of Washington, Secretary of Labor Elaine Chao, Secretary of Transportation Norman Mineta, and Assistant to Secretary of Defense Philip Yun. Conspicuous for its absence is leadership in State and Federal Educational Organizations. Upon examination, perhaps many such assignments may be found in municipal and the District of Columbia systems.

It is interesting to note the nearly uniform political orientation of the various Asian American groups. See the chart below:

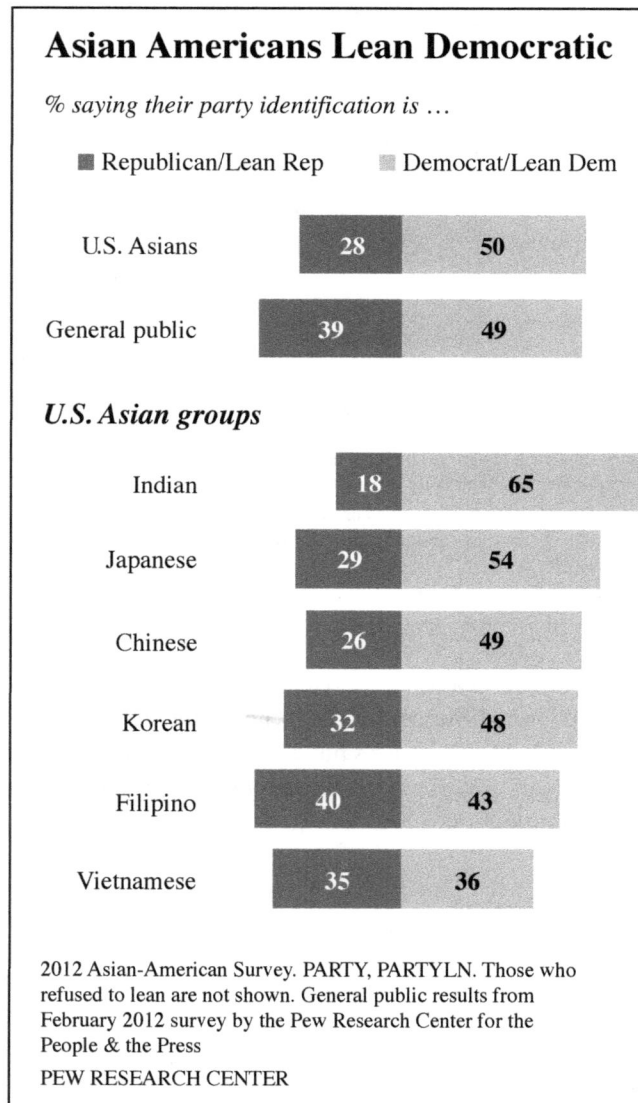

Asian Americans Lean Democratic

% saying their party identification is …

■ Republican/Lean Rep ▨ Democrat/Lean Dem

	Republican/Lean Rep	Democrat/Lean Dem
U.S. Asians	28	50
General public	39	49

U.S. Asian groups

	Republican/Lean Rep	Democrat/Lean Dem
Indian	18	65
Japanese	29	54
Chinese	26	49
Korean	32	48
Filipino	40	43
Vietnamese	35	36

2012 Asian-American Survey. PARTY, PARTYLN. Those who refused to lean are not shown. General public results from February 2012 survey by the Pew Research Center for the People & the Press

PEW RESEARCH CENTER

From "Rise of Asian Americans" by Pew Research Center - Social & Demographic Trends. Copyright © 2012 by Pew Research Center. Reprinted by permission.

Korean Americans

Korean immigration to the U.S. has occurred in basically three waves: The Old Immigration Period (1903–19490, The Intermediate Immigration Period (1946–1964) and the Contemporary Immigration Period (1965–present). In his research at Queens College, CUNY, Pyong Gap Min noted that in spite of these three significant stages, there were others that depict a clear picture of the evolution of Korean immigration to the United States. The transformations reveal the push-pull factors, which prompted the rise, the decline, and the leveling off of Koreans' desire to emigrate. Among the predominant causes for each phase of immigration was clamor for improved educational opportunities. There were certainly other

According to Min, the First Immigration Period was precipitated by "a small number of Koreans, mostly students and politicians" (Min, "Koreans' Immigration" 2), who came to the United States at the end of the nineteenth century. Already the infusion of students was to be felt as the result of the need for educational opportunities and the tendency of the United States to accept immigrants on the basis of perceived national needs. The latter group of Koreans who immigrated came to Hawaii to work the sugar plantations. The move to Hawaii to serve as cheap labor was greatly influenced by concurrent economic issues and famines in Korea. The Chinese Exclusion Act of 1882 had a negative effect on Korean immigration as well as the Chinese. Although the California Gold Rush saw a large increase in Chinese migration in 1848-1949, the Chinese Exclusion of 1882 curtailed Chinese immigration. Korean workers were brought in to offset the activities of Chinese workers who protested horrible working conditions and organized work stoppages. Japan, which was a dominant force in the region at the time, discouraged the migration of Korean workers to Hawaii to protect the demand for Japanese workers. Japan controlled Korea from 1910 to 1945, when it was defeated in World War Two. Those Korean political refugees and students were situated on the Eastern Seaboard, especially New York, and attended mostly Ivy League Universities. At that time the Korean population on the west Coast was minimal, a condition which was to change in the futures of Los Angeles, San Francisco, and Hawaii. The preparation and training, which was acquired in the United States was to have significant impact on and for those Koreans who, after the war, returned to Korea to become political and educational activists.

During The Intermediate Period, (1950–1964), remarkable changes were in store for Korea in general, and South Korea in particular. This was a time when I spent a significant amount of time in Korea and had unremarkable impact on what was to become its legacy. I was able, however, to observe some of the salient features of a relatively undeveloped (at that time and by U. S. standards) country, which had a history beyond which I could imagine. One of the extraordinary features of what seemed like a desolate existence was the strong emphasis on the education of the children. The impact of this characteristic is to be seen throughout the evolution of this journey from Korea's earlier history through contemporary times. It is highly symptomatic of Korean culture wherever it resides. Because of its close relationship with the U. S., immigration to this country has been commonplace, which constitutes a symbiotic relationship as the needs of both the Koreans and the U.S., by virtue of its dependence on the skills brought in by the Koreans, are satisfied. The U. S. has typically not had a problem with groups that mind their business and do not cause disruption, groups that are dedicated to showing passivity with patriotism. The skills that are brought in include, stereotypically, math and science exceptionalities. Sometimes stereotypes are valid and sometimes they are fallacious. Because of the heavy emphasis on study habits, career aspirations, and competitiveness (in a non-competitive culture) achievement in these areas is known to be higher than average. And so the stereotype is perpetuated over time. We must be reminded, though, that stereotypes, positive or negative, can be dangerous for those who do not fit them. Since our culture tends to make judgments about individuals based upon appearances, we are especially susceptible to error in judgment.

For a while, after and during the Korean War (1950–1953), many Korean immigrants were women, most of whom were married to U. S. servicemen in South Korea. In addition, many immigrants were Korean orphans adopted by U. S. servicemen or American citizens. For a while there was a run on American families adopting children of Asian descent and, at the time, considerable speculation as to what the motivation was for the adoptions. Some guessed that it was about salvaging the lives of sometimes-abandoned children from a war-torn country that left us responsible for the residue. Some were thought to feel that because of the stereotype of Asians being exceptionally intelligent, it would be fashionable to have one in the family. After all, an intelligent child would be a positive reflection on the family. It was interesting to observe how the craze subsided after a spell, as fads tend to do.

In time, the emphasis shifted to the emigration of males who were involved in university studies. Korean's historical concentration on education shone through at all age levels, a condition which did not diminish with immigration. Those who emigrate do so forearmed with high levels of academic acuity. The more recent immigrants come armed with mastery of the English language, which makes educational pursuits in American schools not only feasible, but a likely precursor to success on a competitive level. As with all other immigrants, acquisition of English skills is a prerequisite for economic success. In recent decades, American educational institutions have taken great strides towards accommodating enrichment of both native and non-native students at all levels of teaching and learning. Children begin learning foreign languages at the elementary level and continue to do so through high school. In the distant past, most American schools introduced rudimentary levels of Spanish, but little else. Eventually, subjects such as French and German were interjected and were actually taken seriously. Colleges and universities began in the early 1970s to offer ethnic studies programs routinely, which acquainted some students with accompanying languages. Depending upon perceptions of what cultures are becoming significant, especially in the area of global economics, students are likely to be attracted to languages deemed relevant. South Korea is fast becoming a major economic entity that must be dealt with on a global scale. The language, and therefore the culture, is attracting increasing amounts of attention as a major player in the world marketplace. This is an interesting phenomenon regarding a typically low-profile ethnic group in American society. The literature, research, and the Internet abound with information on the relation between this vital group in our society and systems of education, which have played an important part in its development.

The Contemporary Immigration Period for Korean Americans saw a far greater number of immigrants coming to the United States. In fact, almost all of today's Korean Americans immigrated after the Immigration Act of 1965, which changed the landscape and disposed of the previous laws that virtually precluded all but Northeastern Europeans. The large numbers of Asian immigrants were primarily from Third World countries and, thus, tended to be worse-off economically than their Northeastern European counterparts. They were less educated, but a large part of their determination to come to this country involved aspirations for not only work that was better paying, but also educational opportunities. At this time, then, immigrants from Third World countries outnumbered those from economically viable ones.

The Accelerating Period, which occurred between 1965- and 1990, involved increased concern for economic stability (high unemployment rate in Korea beginning in 1998), political instability, and educational opportunities. The push factor was increasing in strength due to what was perceived growing dictator rule, especially in the North. The potential for regional war is ever present, a condition that is growing at this writing. South Korea is an extremely important military ally for the United States, especially from a strategic standpoint. It is both a gateway and a buffer between China, which is seen as a threat to the west, and Japan, which is also an important ally strategically situated in the region. The ever-present military threat is second only to the desire for better education and economic potential for their children. Korean parents are eager to have their children adopted by Americans for that reason. They are prepared to have them placed in American homes and are willing to defray whatever costs are involved. The importance of education continues to be a major driving force in all of the immigration periods for Koreans.

Characteristics of U.S. Korean Adults, 2010

% (unless otherwise noted)

	U.S. Total	U.S. Asians	U.S. Koreans
Foreign born	15.8	74.1	78.5
Of these, arrived in past 10 years	26.3	28.8	24.3
Citizen	91.4	69.6	67.3
Median age *(in years)*	45	41	40
Married	51.4	59.0	55.7
Fertility (women ages 18–44)			
Had a birth in the past 12 months	7.1	6.8	5.2
Of these, % unmarried	37.1	14.6	9.3
Educational attainment (ages 25+)			
Less than high school	14.4	13.9	7.7
High school or more	85.6	86.1	92.3
Bachelor's degree or more	28.2	49.0	52.6
Median annual personal earnings			
Full-time, year-round workers	$40,000	$48,000	$45,000
Household annual income			
Median	$49,800	$66,000	$50,000
Average household size *(persons)*	2.6	3.1	2.6
Homeownership rate	65.4	58.1	48.1
In poverty	12.8	11.9	15.1
Language			
Speaks English "very well"	90.4	63.5	54.0
Speaks English less than "very well"	9.6	36.5	46.0
Region of residence			
Northeast	18.3	20.1	21.3
Midwest	21.6	11.3	11.3
South	37.0	21.5	22.8
West	23.0	47.1	44.6

Note: Unmarried women include those who are divorced, separated, widowed or never married. "High school or more" includes those who attained at least a high school diploma or an equivalent, such as a General Education Development (GED) certificate. "Speaks English 'very well'" includes those who speak only English at home. U.S. Asians and U.S. Koreans include mixed-race and mixed-group populations, regardless of Hispanic origin.

Source: Pew Research Center analysis of 2010 American Community Survey, Integrated Public Use Microdata Sample (IPUMS) files

PEW RESEARCH CENTER

From "Rise of Asian Americans" by Pew Research Center - Social & Demographic Trends. Copyright © 2012 by Pew Research Center. Reprinted by permission.

Filipino Americans

Filipino Americans are a group that was initially brought in specifically to serve as laborers in farms and fish canneries in Seattle and Alaska. In my cultural anthropology classes I have encouraged students to investigate the history, the culture, and the sometimes tepid relationship between the United States and the Philippine Islands. There is often curiosity about the convergence of native cultural characteristics and the influence of Spanish roots. The curiosity often revolves around the question of "what is the basis of the use of Spanish names?" The Filipinos spoke some Spanish and some Tagalong, for they were described as Tagalas. The United States maintained colonial rule over the Philippines from 1898 to 1946, but Filipinos were not granted citizenship. Like other Asian groups, Filipinos were accused of taking jobs away from Whites and suppressing wages. Congress restricted Filipino immigration to fifty people per year between the Great Depression and the aftermath of World War II (Kendall 265).

As the result of the Immigration Act of 1965, Filipinos with higher levels of education, such as physicians, nurses, technical workers and other professionals, moved to the U. S. mainland. On a practical level, people may notice in their daily routines the inordinate number of Filipinos who are employed in the areas of health services (at all levels) and accounting. If they do not get services as high as physicians, it is likely that they will receive services of nurses. The push-pull factor comes into play as low pay in the Philippines coincides with ongoing nurse shortages in the United States. Filipino nurses formed The Filipino Nurses Association in New York in 1928. A large community of Filipinos settled in California producing a Filipino nursing population of twenty percent of all nurses. Without start-up capital, many could not open their own businesses and have been employed in low-wage service occupations. Kendall notes, however, that Filipinos, according to Napholz and Mo, have among the highest level of educational attainment among Asian Americans, and Filipino American households have above-average income, in part because they tend to have more workers per family and pool their income (qtd. in Kendall 265).

All of the Filipino immigrants were not poor or uneducated. In fact, some came to the U. S. for educational reasons. A group called *pensionados* were middle class government scholars who entered for the purpose of furthering their education in the United States. Many then returned home after schooling and training, but most of the migrant workers remained in the United States. The *pensionados,* who were funded by their government, were required to contribute a like amount of time and service to the country once they returned, similar to the educational grants once allocated to students in the U.S. who majored in either education or the sciences. Once finished, they were required to serve in their field for a period commensurate with their grant period. Often, some of the returning *pensionados* were disparaged by their countrymen for having a haughty attitude after becoming Americanized. At the beginning of World War II, Filipinos were barred from serving in the military. In 1942, President Franklin Roosevelt allowed them to be drafted. Many served side-by-side with other American servicemen and women. However, my experiences aboard Navy ships in the Korean War revealed that practically all of the stewards, who were actually servants for the White officers. In fact, I never witnessed other than Filipino stewards. My Birmingham, Alabama upbringing made me conscious of such things.

Vietnamese Americans

Vietnamese Americans are perhaps the "new kid on the Block" among Asian Americans. The greatest influx of Southeastern Asians did not occur until as late as 1975 at the fall of Saigon, ending the war in Vietnam. The fact that this war was not a typical "win" for the U.S. did not make the acceptance of these mostly refugees easier. Rightfully, the U.S. Government for whatever reason has taken some responsibility for their demise and has provided for their accommodation in the safety of the United States. Many had to flee Vietnam out of fear of the communist party so that the exit for them was not pleasant and certainly was not a matter of choice. Serious adjustments must be made to accommodate the introduction of this people to an alien culture. Adjustments have to be made by both the immigrants and the existing society. The adjustment for Americans has been gradual and difficult. Much of the resentment stems from the price paid in both life and treasure by the U. S. during the war. The clash of cultures has also been a major factor in the difficult adjustment.

The fact that the second wave of Vietnamese emigration in 1977 was about the power and influence of the communist party is a definitive indication of just who prevailed in that war. Businesses were confiscated. Citizens were relocated to rural, uncultivated areas. Those suspected of being loyal to South Vietnam were tortured and "reeducated" to communist principles. This "push" factor was strong and growing in intensity. Much of the accommodation was generated via voluntary organizations and churches. Vietnamese families were provided food, shelter, and other basic necessities by sponsors, who were responsible for helping them adjust to American life. They were responsible for helping refugees seek employment and enrolling their children in school. All of these efforts were about assimilating this new group to American values. The government, as it is wont to do, did not look closely enough at the social and geographic needs of these new people. We watched in amazement as the stream of Vietnamese descended on Orange County, California. Their first entry points were spread about in such refugee centers as Arkansas, Pennsylvania, and Florida. Two important considerations were not dealt with that would have profound impact on the location of choice for the refugees. The social consideration was about family. People choose to live with and around people they know. The geographic consideration had mostly to do with climate. The Vietnamese were not accustomed to cold weather. The immigrants soon realized that both family and climate concerns could be solved in Southern California, where some refugees had landed. The consequence of this realization is that today forty percent of all Vietnamese live in Orange County, California, where a large enclave called "Little Saigon" resides.

Two principle values among this new immigrant group are family ties and education. Education has been the vehicle making inroads into higher status occupations. The Vietnamese consider American education to be prestigious, compared to their own institution, especially in the areas of technology and science. They are heavily enrolled in American community colleges and are the third largest country of origin in the community colleges after Korea and Japan. Rectifying the earlier problem of slow-paced economic and career advancement did not come easily. The issue of poor language skills has dogged other immigrant groups as well as they sought to climb the status ladder. The key is, and always has been, for the group to recognize the importance of acquiring the host country's native language and then setting out to gain the necessary skills to function at a viable level in the important facets of society. After making the initial rather painful adjustments, the Vietnamese have gained a strong foothold in politics and in managerial and professional fields, primarily due to their educational attainment. Early on, they were said to be the fifth largest Asian immigrant group behind Chinese, Filipino, Asian Indian, and Korean. In 2010 they became the second largest such group.

East Indians

As was mentioned earlier in this book, no immigrant group has joined this society without major difficulties, some worse than others. The East Indians are no exception. They have managed to fly under the radar in recent times, but their journey has been fraught with pitfalls brought on simply by being different. Even in contemporary times most modern day Americans are not aware of that journey. Because we rely so much on stereotypes in decision-making about others, the first assumption that comes to mind regarding East Indians is that their role is in the customer service venue and that all customer service calls will be redirected to India where the agents have few English skills. However, upon closer examination East Indian immigrants are far more than that. For example, they come to the United States better educated than all of their other Asian counterparts. Many of those possessing medium to high levels of education come from the privileged classes, which meant access to educational opportunities both at home and abroad. There is, however, the matter of East Indians who suffered the indignities of slavery both abroad and in the United States. Some of the first East Asians were imported to the United States via England as indentured laborers, a result of England's domination of India in the 19th Century. Some were required to serve as servants for their sea-faring captains. They also served as laborers to the West Indies colonies. In viewing some of Virginia's history, there is ample evidence of East Indian slavery in Colonial Chesapeake.

In spite of the humble beginnings in Virginia, Asian Americans have done very well economically, educationally, and professionally. Note the following regarding median household income and college degree or higher:

Sampler of Key Demographic and Survey Findings

% of adults (unless otherwise noted)

	Median household income	College degree or higher*	Foreign born	Recent inter-marriage rate	Majority or plurality religion	Satisfied with life	Satisfied with direction of country	Personal finances (Excellent/ Good)	Belief in hard work**
U.S. Asians	$66,000	49	74	29	Christian	82	43	51	69
General public	$49,800	28	16	15	Christian	75	21	35	58
U.S. Asian groups									
Chinese	$65,050	51	76	26	Unaffiliated	84	41	55	61
Filipino	$75,000	47	69	48	Catholic	82	30	50	72
Indian	$88,000	70	87	12	Hindu	84	47	67	75
Vietnamese	$53,400	26	84	18	Buddhist	82	56	29	83
Korean	$50,000	53	78	32	Protestant	83	48	45	64
Japanese	$65,390	46	32	55	*No Plurality*	81	36	57	59

* ages 25 and older
** share that agrees that "most people who want to get ahead can make it if they're willing to work hard"

Source: The four items to the left are from Pew Research Center analysis of 2010 American Community Survey, Integrated Public Use Microdata Sample (IPUMS) files. The five items to the right are from the Pew Research Center 2012 Asian-American Survey.

PEW RESEARCH CENTER

Characteristics of U.S. Indian Adults, 2010

% (unless otherwise noted)

	U.S. Total	U.S. Asians	U.S. Indians
Foreign born	15.8	74.1	87.2
Of these, arrived in past 10 years	26.3	28.8	37.6
Citizen	91.4	69.6	56.2
Median age *(in years)*	45	41	37
Married	51.4	59.0	70.9
Fertility (women ages 18–44)			
Had a birth in the past 12 months	7.1	6.8	8.4
Of these, % unmarried	37.1	14.6	2.3
Educational attainment (ages 25+)			
Less than high school	14.4	13.9	9.2
High school or more	85.6	86.1	90.8
Bachelor's degree or more	28.2	49.0	70.0
Median annual personal earnings			
Full-time, year-round workers	$40,000	$48,000	$65,000
Household annual income			
Median	$49,800	$66,000	$88,000
Average household size *(persons)*	2.6	3.1	3.1
Homeownership rate	65.4	58.1	56.7
In poverty	12.8	11.9	9.0
Language			
Speaks English "very well"	90.4	63.5	76.2
Speaks English less than "very well"	9.6	36.5	23.8
Region of residence			
Northeast	18.3	20.1	31.1
Midwest	21.6	11.3	16.8
South	37.0	21.5	28.5
West	23.0	47.1	23.5

Note: Unmarried women include those who are divorced, separated, widowed or never married. "High school or more" includes those who attained at least a high school diploma or an equivalent, such as a General Education Development (GED) certificate. "Speaks English 'very well'" includes those who speak only English at home. U.S. Asians and U.S. Indians include mixed-race and mixed-group populations, regardless of Hispanic origin.

Source: Pew Research Center analysis of 2010 American Community Survey, Integrated Public Use Microdata Sample (IPUMS) files

PEW RESEARCH CENTER

History indicates that the passage from India to the United States has not always been a pleasant one. One wonders why even some of the Brahmins in Indian would see the need to forsake their privileged positions to venture into a young and uncertain future across the "Black Sea" to America. Sociologically, it is generally believed that the better a person is prepared educationally, the easier it is to make necessary adjustments to changes in options and social status. The willingness to take chances is not so daunting when the person has already experienced some measure of success, especially educationally. Career opportunities were rumored to be significantly greater in the United States, and the pay was as least twice as much as in India. Those who are not as well prepared and flexible would not risk taking chances that could lose everything. And then there is the matter of being able to fund one's passage to uncertainty.

Though most East Asians generally were not as reliant on the American delivery system as most other immigrants, they used the foundation of what skills they possessed to enhance their academic standing to enviable levels. We must not, however, forget that not everyone was so well endowed educationally and that provisions are still necessary to ameliorate deficiencies. From early on, there have been laborers, farm workers, and loggers whose children need to be acclimated to American education.

Today, Asian Indians are distributed throughout the United States, with the largest percentage situated in California, followed by New York. The numbers tend to get smaller as we look Eastward, beginning with the Midwest. To a great extent, the distribution may be attributed to economic opportunities as perceived by the immigrants. As an African American, it is difficult to understand why circumstances such as the history of acceptance levels would not be strong considerations. Even today, with all of the changes that have occurred with regards to race relations, there are areas in this nation that, given the option, I would choose to avoid. This is obviously indication that newer generations are not saddled with those previous conditions.

THE UNIQUENESS OF ETHNICITY

Too often, the concepts of ethnicity and race are used interchangeably. They are not the same, but sometimes are confused because they are used in the same context and because the two concepts can be used to relate to the same group. Whereas any definition of race necessarily refers to biological or physical characteristics, ethnicity describes the cultural aspects of a group, such as the clothing, music, religion, food, rituals, and language valued and used by a group. And though the two sometimes overlap, the distinction is an important one. This is especially true now that there is such an amalgamation of physical characteristics in U. S. society, which only serves to confuse the matter even more. Most Americans see this condition to be the wave of the future. The last election brought this matter to the fore as it was realized that the demographics of the U.S. is fast evolving to a more comprehensive population. Ethnicity is not a new concept. However, it has seemed to take on a new level of significance in recent decades. In a society that claims to be accepting of all interest groups, there seems to be a withdrawal into exclusivity based upon pride in the nature of one's own group. In the effort to be seen as Americanized, or in the process of becoming so, groups often have suppressed their normal dispositions in order to gain the acceptance of the majority. The prevailing attitude of majority groups too often is "the closer you resemble us, or the more you are in the process of becoming like us, the more acceptable you are." Acceptance has been an important goal as groups attempt to navigate themselves through progression.

A heightened sense of ethnicity does not translate to denigrating the national identity as some have proposed. Rather, the tendency to "circle the wagons" and solidify group identity most often happens as the result of being isolated by the larger society. And yet there is still the need to feel that all are part of the whole. Majority group values are typically embraced by minority groups in the effort to be a participant in the society at large. Identity with group values very often occurs as a defense mechanism in addition to ethnic pride for pride's sake. We have come more and more to comprehend the effects of bullying and exclusion. In the past such treatment was perceived to simply be what growing up is all about. "Everyone is subjected to it in one form or another" is not a legitimate excuse for victimizing others. Fortunately, we now understand what the long-term psychological and sociological effects can be in people's lives. This phenomenon is no less serious for the groups that make up society. Exclude the group, and it is likely to retire from normal participation into a defensive mode. With the recent school shootings at all levels, the results for several teenagers who felt excluded from routine involvement in social activities have been devastating for society.

Another indication that ethnicity is not necessarily about race is the treatment of the Bosnian Muslims by the Serbs in the so-called "ethnic cleansing" in Bosnia and Herzegovina. The "cleansing" involved murder, torture, false arrests and imprisonment, rape, removal, and deportation. There were no "ethnic minorities" as they are often defined in our society. There were no "people of color," a term often used derogatorily in our society to categorize anyone who is not White. So, how could there be ethnic groups? It's because ethnicity does not mean race. Never mind that the fortunes reversed themselves to some extent as the Muslims and Croats returned the favor against the Bosnians to a lesser extent.

To further distinguish between race and ethnicity, and to ensure that race does not confuse the issue, consider a group defined as "White Ethnics" in the United States, the largest of German descent. Farley says that they are "a wide variety of groups from Eastern and Southern Europe, including Italian, Polish, Czech, Hungarian, Greek, and Ukrainian Americans. Besides their geographic origins, two other important features distinguish these groups from the rest of the white population. First, they are more recent immigrants. Most of them came between the late nineteenth century and the imposition of immigration quotas in 1924. Northern and Western European immigrants, in contrast, came a good deal earlier. Second, unlike earlier immigrants, almost none of the "white ethnics" was Protestant, the dominant religious group in the United States" (Farley 324). A good example of the effects of these dynamics as they impact the lives of new immigrants is the treatment of the Irish immigrants who were subjected to harsh discriminatory practices in every aspect of their daily lives. The existing Protestant White majority was not accepting of new immigrants who were not of their faith. Another serious consideration that worked against the new arrivals was the view that they were a threat to desirable jobs. As we look at problems for new immigrants in general, real or imagined, the issue of jobs is a constant.

Ethnicity can be as significant a deterrent to harmony among groups as the concept of race. Obviously, a combination of the two can devastate the functionality of a society. However, this is not necessarily so. There are societies that exist in harmony while embracing ethnic differences. One of the most outstanding examples of intergroup harmony within a country is Switzerland, where "a variety of ethnic and language groups have gotten along in relative harmony for years"(Farley 312). There are four languages spoken. Each is considered important in its own right. All four cultural groups are equally represented in the government. Theirs is the best example of what multiculturalism is all about. We in the U. S. define ourselves as multicultural, but a closer look reveals a culture where all groups are not equally represented beyond written government policy. Also, all languages spoken in the country are not equally valued. According to Farley, "In Hawaii, racial diversity is greater than anywhere else in the United States—no race is a majority there—and interracial relations, though far from perfect, are in general more harmonious than elsewhere in the United States" (Farley 312).

The point is that the tensions seen and felt across the mainland United States are not necessary. I have suggested, perhaps out of ignorance, that the United States is the perfect laboratory for instituting racial and ethnic understanding and cooperation, for the diversity is unlike any other nation on earth. Although people tend to fear the unknown, the nature of American society necessarily requires some contact or at least cyber knowledge of other groups that inhabit this nation. So, there should be no unknown, unless individuals choose to isolate themselves from the world around them. This is a situation that often produces sociopaths and psychopaths.

Ethnicity can also be a very positive force, for it can provide for group cohesion and solidarity, which is healthy when applied in a way favorable to society's well-being. Racists have given ethnicity a bad name. In the absence of support and recognition from external groups, group cohesion may provide the last-ditch effort for sustainability. The downside of ethnicity is the sense that one is relegated to a position in society based solely on some arbitrary designation provided by others. Resulting anguish can cause anger, resentment, and withdrawal from mainstream society, which does not serve a progressive purpose for anyone. It remains to be seen if ethnic awareness will prove to be a positive fact of life or an impediment to social consonance. Often self-concept relies on group affinity and support to sustain viability. In the absence of recognition from without, acknowledgement from within is crucial to one's well-being.

HOW RACE AND ETHNICITY INTERSECT

Race and ethnicity are often confused because there are commonalities that inevitably blend situations that concern both. Categorization is a tool customarily used in our society—unwisely and often with destructive results. Differences in physical appearances are easily discerned, but not very easily interpreted. As was mention previously, monumental errors are routinely made regarding individual's membership in a particular interest group. The designation may be absolutely insignificant to the matter at hand and may cause irrevocable harm to one's person or reputation. In addition, it very often deprives individuals of rights and opportunities guaranteed to all. Judgment of this sort too often is based upon an individual's or group's, personal outlook and perhaps past experiences with persons with similar physical appearances. The inability to interpret the evolution of the racial make-up of our society is a burden that younger generations should be able to avoid. It is clear to me in my classes that this is definitely the case, for the most part. Obviously, race is still a factor in American society, but not to the extent of the past. The concept is abhorrent to most of the young people. Like other orientations that have held us captive in the past, such as communism and religious differences, society is reaching a level of sophistication that raises the bar, and we fear only those things that deserve to be feared. Of course, fear is on a continuum and is subject to change with societal change.

Ethnicity presents a more difficult problem for us, for identifying it is far more elusive. It has become more and more difficult to identify a person's ethnicity at a glance because in the past the determination was made simply on the basis of physical appearance. Since the civil rights movement, which I contend freed all groups to be what they wanted to be, horrible mistakes in judgments have occurred in important situations, such as hiring practices, home mortgages, and education. Prejudgment means just that, making decisions about individuals without benefit of the facts. The laziness of our society makes us prone to attempt to judgments based on stereotypes. In today's society, little can be more erroneous. The laziness results from desiring to deal with individuals as members of groups, as opposed to distinct individuals. It takes too much effort when we've got the code right before us.

Race and ethnicity will continue to dog us, but as time passes it will become increasingly manageable. Noted sociologist, William Wilson, says that today the concept of race is subjugated to social class (qtd. in Kendall 252). For example, African Americans are far more likely to interact with other African Americans of the same social class than those in other social classes. Across the social class structure, classes can relate to the circumstances of a class position in society if they have had the same experiences.

Part Five

An Aging Population and Education

The United States is experiencing what is sometimes called "The Graying of America," which insinuates different meaning depending upon one's perspective. It is a blessing for those who embrace longevity for longevity's sake. Conversely, the aging process can wreak havoc on individuals and their loved ones in dealing with debilitating injuries or illnesses. Good longevity is longevity accompanied by sound physical and mental health. Longevity is increasing by leaps and bounds in the U.S., coupled with little preparation in the form of work and social activities. In the not-too-distant past, older citizens were also defined as "poor." Because of programs such as social security benefits, that problem has been adequately addressed. But the big question today is "what do we do with the old folks?" How do we address the issue from their perspective? How are they to be involved in relevant pursuits? If anyone has noticed lately, they are not going away voluntarily. This causes a bottleneck in the job market, especially at the higher end, which causes friction between the newer generations and the old. In recent times some people have considered retraining older workers towards new meaningful occupations. Most are not willing to regress to tasks that are not challenging to their capabilities.

Ageism is defined as discriminating against persons on the basis of age. While we tend to automatically see this contemptible behavior focused on older people, it also applies to such treatment of the young. Though our society is more youth oriented than most, younger people pay a price for not having attained a more "respectful" station in life, as have their seniors. Older persons are subjected to all kinds of indignities primarily due the stereotypes applied to them. As we mentioned before, stereotypes can be both valid and misleading. The major problem is the difficulty in determining which is which. Stereotypes often defy logic. But they seem justified because they are shared with others who seem logical. At issue is the tendency to not question the validity of stereotypes. So they are perpetuated over vast amounts of time, tending to eventually resemble "truth."

As we view the changing nature of older people in American society, we see the need for certain new accommodations for them. We have erroneously thought of education being unique to young people. But throughout history, education has been important to all of society. Originally, informal education was conducted at the knee of one's parents. Then came the sophistication of growth and the expansion of technological concerns, albeit at rudimentary levels. This called for the development of formal education, which would require uniformity in delivery systems. Still, the emphasis was primarily on the education of society's children. This makes some sense, since forward-looking societies see children to be their future. However, what was forgotten in the equation, are the needs of a growing number of seniors who wish to remain relevant. The relatively new discussion of those needs involves "Life Long Learning," a concept that seeks to address evolving interests of seniors, as well as others. According to Appelbaum and Chambliss,

> *American culture is beginning to recognize the importance of lifelong earning for the elderly, although little is yet being done through government programs. Growing numbers of elderly people will avail themselves of educational opportunities of all sorts, from university "emeriti education" programs for senior citizens to continuing or adult education programs on local college campuses. Some American corporations provide educational and training programs for their older workers, and early retirement programs, sometimes termed* golden parachutes *or* golden handshakes, *enable a small number of people (mainly upper middle class) to develop*

*second careers after retiring from their principal work. Yet relatively few such programs exist for
the vast majority of elderly retirees (Appelbaum and Chambliss 346).*

The significance of remaining relevant is crucial to the elderly outlook on life. It is no secret that it becomes more and more difficult to keep abreast of changing dynamics in society as we grow older. This is most transparent in the areas of technology, the political landscape, and acquiring new language skills, such as Adult Basic Education (ABE) and English for speakers of other languages (ESOL). Some elderly people are more capable of evolving with changing social phenomena than others, but they tend to be in the minority. Nevertheless, that minority is impressive, for they exhibit the willingness to venture into the unknown, however uncomfortable. Their message is "We're not quite done yet. We won't be left totally behind." This means that social policy has to include accommodations for extending educational opportunities beyond those for young people. Many institutions, especially community colleges, have instituted adult education components to address this emerging need. Even in mainstream classes today, it is not unusual to find a few more mature students sitting among the traditional younger ones. I have noticed in my own classes that older students generally outperform the younger ones. Generally. Intervening factors may include such things as life experiences, maturity, missed previous opportunity, and dedication to the academic task.

So, what are some of the considerations for delivering successful educational programs to older people? Most often there is no need to do anything different from what is done for students at large. It is generally said that the age of the instructor should not be a factor in an age-integrated setting. But the relevance of the experience level can indeed be a factor. Marcus and Havighurst refer to the 1970 *Handbook of Adult Education*: "'This is a time for educational revolution—a time when adults of all ages and from all walks of life are returning to the education they missed when they were of "school age"' (Cortwright and Brice, 1970, p. 407)" (22). They go on to explain:

> *The addition of men and women of advanced years to the new clientele of education was signaled
> at the 1971 White House Conference on Aging, where the delegates declared, "Education is a basic
> right of all persons of all age groups. It is continuous and therefore one of the ways of enabling
> older people to have a full and meaningful life, and a means of helping them develop their potential
> as a resource for the betterment of society"(1971 White House conference on Aging, 1973, p. 6). (22)*

Regarding personnel, Marcus and Havighurst state further in "Education for the Aging":

> *In courses offered as part of the regular curricula of the sponsoring institution, it is customary to
> integrate students of all ages in the classes and to use the services of regularly employed instruc-
> tors, regardless of their age, Programs established especially for older adults usually are kept
> age-segregated, but their teachers may be any age. It is desirable now and will become increas-
> ingly important in the future that the training of teachers of adults also include exposure to ger-
> ontology to assure greater sensitivity to the physical and social attributes of aging, for example,
> the slowing of physiological response time and impaired self-esteem in some persons." (41)*

They also explode a myth regarding the characteristics of older learners. It is counterproductive to enter into providing educational services to senior citizens with preconceived notions about their learning potential, their physical acuity, and their interests. According to Marcus and Havighurst,

> *Experience in conducting programs for mixed-age groups has tended to undermine still another
> prevalent notion, that age categories are mutually incompatible in the classroom. Studies of
> generational value structures suggest that the young and the old resemble each other in their
> attitudes more than either may resemble the generation between. There are numerous examples
> of youth welcoming the presence and participation of older-aged persons in their activities. A
> developing type of adult education activity is the intergenerational encounter workshop involv-
> ing planned dialogue among members of three or more generations, which provides a means for
> each to examine and redefine human and social attitudes. It offers promise as a useful tool for
> training and educating personnel in the helping professions." (45)*

I have noticed in my classes that the young and older students have very much in common, relative to values. Sometimes the outcome is positive and sometimes not. Both groups tend to emanate from the same communities, which share the same social and political values, many of which are embedded in the culture over generations without debate. Mix-aged classrooms are excellent venues for displaying different points of view.

While policy makers have not kept pace with educational needs of the elderly, they have begun the process with some measure of success. The impetus for improvement has come primarily from the people who would be most impacted – the elderly. Powerful activist organizations, such as The Gray Panthers and the American Association of Retired Persons (AARP), have sprung up throughout the country to have influence on legislative affairs and exercise other political influence. The AARP is one of the most powerful lobbying groups in the nation's capital. These organizations are certain to keep a watchful eye on developing educational requirements of older citizens. Much of the change in attitude regarding the elderly has to do with this sort of organization, but also due to the increase in longevity and the increase in their numbers. They are not only more numerous, but also armed with more economic power. It was not that long ago that older people were defined as poverty stricken. Because of the effects of Social Security and other federal programs, that is no longer the case. In order for progress to continue, public policy will necessarily have to persist in its efforts. The growth in the elderly population is expected to skyrocket by the year 2050. There are indications that the trend has already begun. The term **graying of America** refers to this growing percentage of older people in the U. S. population. . . . In 1900, only 4 percent of Americans were age 65 or older. Today, 13 percent are. (Henslin 362).

An important impediment to society responding adequately to older people's needs is the misunderstanding of where they are in their lives. Too often we rely on stereotypes to guide our comprehension. Most of the stereotypes of older people are way off the mark, but the presumptions emanating from them have as much impact as if they were valid. What are some of the common stereotypes and how might misconceptions be dispelled? I refer the reader to pages 198-200 in my book, "There Are Always Blue Skies . . . Over the Dark Clouds", 2nd ed., to get some possible responses to people's hackneyed ideas about seniors. Some of their notions:

"Old people talk too much." Response—maybe they are desperate for interaction. People generally do not want to spend extended time with them.

"Old people are whiners and are too dependent." Response—quite the contrary. Older people typically don't want anything from the young. Our job is to get you to be independent, at which time we feel that we've done our job.

"Yeah, but old people are stingy." Response—Try growing up in The Depression years. Try to imagine the fear of outlasting your money.

"And old people stink." Usually, it is more about overindulgence in perfumes for older women and Ben Gay for men, though sometimes the memory processes may fade, and personal hygiene may become secondary to conservative use of fragrances and naps.

"Old people are grumpy and set in their ways." Response—Grumpy could be a result of something hurting or disillusionment with new-fangled ideas. What we know is what is important.

"They can't drive." Response—Yes, there are too many of us who should give it up by now. But that would also mean giving up an important part of our independence, and we're not quite ready for that (West 198–200).

I would hope that younger folks would be a little more tolerant of their seniors, for if they are fortunate, they will someday be there themselves.

Part Six

The Interdependence of Politics and Education

Our political education usually begins at home. Much of what we believe politically results from what is heard around the dinner table, though the implant of ideas may well be unintentional. Of the various socialization agents in our lives, family gets the first shots at us and typically remains influential in our lives. Other socialization agents are schools, religion, close friends, media, sports teams, and social organizations. But these come along later in our lives, by which time the die is cast. One of the most significant intervening factors at that point is likely to be formal education. Much of what has been learned now comes into question, which is a healthy development. In recent times more and more attention has been given to the concept of critical thinking, which means being open to consider multiple possibilities, even if some run counter to one's own thoughts. Max Weber says, "that a key task of sociological inquiry was to openly acknowledge 'inconvenient facts'" (Gerth and Mills as qtd. in Weber 1946).

Education can at once solidify existing orientations or bring into question those that require examination. Irrevocable damage to the potential for progress when inquiry is quashed is always a possibility. As society undergoes inevitable change, social institutions necessarily must make adjustments if they are to remain relevant and functional. In the recent presidential election, when only about fifty percent of eligible voters voted, all political parties, both major and minor, learned a number of lessons about the evolution of American society. The hesitance employed by one party revealed a party in denial. In spite of some efforts to correct the party's projection, there are likely to be long-term political consequences.

What is the impact of education on political activity? The lower the educational attainment, the less likely individuals are to be involved in politics, even when they have the legal right to participate. The rationale for non-involvement is likely to involve the feeling that political outcomes will not matter to them because the powers that be will do whatever they choose anyway. Another rationale is that they are not knowledgeable enough about the issues to express themselves politically. While there may be some truth to their latter concern, the same applies, too often, to young potential voters. Too often the perception of some is that the political system is not for them. In fact, it is seen as a force against them. The solution to the problem is probably too simplistic. First of all, increasingly, the population is becoming more aware that there really is strength in numbers, as indicated vividly by our election. Only recently have some groups become acutely aware of this fact. Secondly, it is incumbent upon those who have the right to vote to become aware of the issues and exercise that right. Obviously, the lower the social class, the less opportunity individuals generally have for access to formal education. This results in the lack of opportunity to interact with others, such as educators and other learners, about contemporary social issues. People who stand to gain most from the system are more likely to vote, for they seek to protect their interests. The lower the social class, the fewer interests there are to protect, resulting in decreased political participation. People tend to vote to their own advantage, assuming that others are doing the same.

Note that the older voters are, the most likely they are to vote. We might speculate that (1) they may be more aware of the issues (I often hear from students that they don't vote because they do not know the particulars), and (2) they vote to protect their own interests, feeling that they have been marginalized.

Females are slightly more likely to vote than males. They depend on the political system to eventually rectify gender inequities, for the social apparatus has not done the job.

African Americans are less likely to vote than the Euro-Americans who have more to protect. They are more likely to vote than the Hispanic population, for they have been in the political forefront for an extended length of time, prior to and continuing with the civil rights movement of the 1960's. The 1964 Civil Rights Act indicated to African Americans that the political process, though very slow, actually could effect social change.

Education is extremely significant in voting trends. The more education, the more voters are likely to understand how the process affects them. They, too, are interested in maintaining their privileged positions in society, and one way to accomplish this is to maintain the distance between themselves and those who are less politically involved. Earning capacity usually directly correlates with education.

Those who are employed are more likely to vote than the unemployed and those not in the labor force. Again, holding ones position in society is often dependent upon being knowledgeable and actively involved in things political.

Note that, in each of the years, college graduates outdistanced all other groups in voting for president, followed by those with some college. It appears that the lower the educational level, the lower the political participation (Henslin 431).

If it can be assumed that those in power do whatever is necessary to maintain their positions, and there is ample evidence of the veracity of the notion, then an important method used to accomplish that goal is the skillful use of the political system. The economic system in the U. S. revolves around the clout held by those who make all of the nation's decisions, large and small. Political decisions impact jobs, educational policy, international affairs, efforts to regulate healthcare programs, and all other issues affecting society's day-to-day requirements. We are sometimes deluded into the belief that we, the people, make those decisions. But the truth is that most are made outside of our sphere of influence. Unfortunately, this is the reason many people feel alienated from the system and feel powerless. It takes a great deal of resolve to persist towards political goals in spite of the odds we face. The resolve is likely to be had by those who are somewhat knowledgeable about social issues and are determined to treat the system as it was designed to be treated. That cadre of citizens is absolutely essential to the good health of the society. Since knowledge is the best defense we have against totalitarianism, the institution of education stands as the most effective fortification against annihilation.

Part Seven

Social Class: The Relative Significance of Education

Professor James Henslin in *Sociology: A Down-To-Earth Approach* offers the following vignette:

> The man was a C student in school. As a businessman, he ran an oil company (Arbusto) into the ground. A self-confessed alcoholic until age forty, he was arrested for drunk driving. With this background, how did he become president of the United States?
>
> Accompanying these personal factors was the power of social class. George W. Bush was born the grandson of a wealthy senator and the son of a businessman who, after serving as a member of the House of Representatives and director of the CIA, was elected president of the United States. For high school, he went to an elite private prep school, Andover; for his bachelor's degree to Yale; and for his MBA to Harvard. He was given $1 million to start his own business. When that business failed, Bush fell softly, landing on the boards of several corporations. Taken care of even further, he was made the managing director of the Texas Rangers baseball team and allowed to buy a share of the team for $600,000, which he sold for $15 million.
>
> When it was time for him to get into politics, Bush's connections financed his run for governor of Texas and then for president. (Henslin 269)

Henslin's issue here is the significance of social class and how it either impedes or enhances one's life chances. As of December 2013, the United States has a population of more than 317 billion people. One would think that of that number, an extremely large proportion would emerge as a pool of eligibles from which the most powerful person on earth might be selected. The intervening factor here is obviously social class, which supersedes all rational thought when it comes to allocating rights and privileges to individuals, regardless of qualifications. I still remain amazed that such a thing could have happened in a fairly sophisticated society that is bulging with political, economic, and academic talent. History will inform us of the long-range effects of Bush's influence on the society.

So who was this man who is defined as a member of the capitalist class? And how does he compare with those who are not so fortunate? In my classes I tell students that I expect them to be alarmed about the unequal distribution of wealth in our society. Most are totally unaware of the discrepancy, so the impact of the revelation is significant. The one percent in the capitalist class is a powerful group and has tremendous influence on the general direction of the society. They are comprised of the "old" money folks who are firmly established and who have distain for those who have not been financially entrenched for very long, and the "new" money variety, sometimes referred to as the "nouveau riche." In both cases, education is a significant factor, but oddly enough, more of a factor for the newcomers than the "old" money group. Groups in all social classes have aspirations to progress into the next higher class. "New" money people have such aspirations and value education as a vehicle to move them ahead. "Old" money people value education also, but not for the same reason. They expect education to help to keep them in their privileged positions. What are absent for them, though, are motivation and the "vehicle" to move them up. They are already there. And in order to maintain the future of their status, they insist on ensuring that their children are "properly" educated. That means that they should attend the "proper" or "best" educational institutions, most often the schools that they themselves have attended. Because of their financial positions, education costs are not an issue, so they can afford to send their children to the costliest schools. I try to remind my students that this may not necessarily translate to the "best" schools because strong consideration must be given the nature of the academic experience. Sometimes the best schools are public institutions with stronger academic emphasis. Sometimes the so-called "proper" schools are more about interacting with like-minded people, people of the same socioeconomic standing.

Education is also a meaningful tool for those in the lower middle-class, for it is their vehicle for moving about at least within the middle class, from lower middle-class, to middle-class, to upper middle-class. Their chances of moving totally out of the middle class are not very good. But the potential is an effective "carrot" to wave before their noses with the promise of unlikely upward mobility. They are, however, in a much better place than their lower class counterparts, who have far less opportunity for both educational and career access. The major factor that affects their movement is economics. There is no way to separate the three things that make up one's status in society: occupation, education, and income.

A large part of the surprise results from students' belief in the party line about equal opportunity for all in their society. We can all probably appreciate the importance of such a doctrine in perpetuating belief in the practicality of our own efforts towards progress. Then I feel the necessity to explain that upward mobility does not live up to its billing. The U.S. follows the United Kingdom and Italy in potential for social class mobility, in spite of our declaration of "opportunity for all," which deceives many believers. Very few individuals will transcend major class boundaries. Fewer than five percent of people will cross major class boundaries. For example, the potential for middle-class persons to move into the upper class is practically nil, the problem being that those who are already there are not receptive to the new arrivals. Of course, the possibility is always there, but the chances are not very good for the majority. The idea continues to be important to society, for it is what makes for the vitality that comes from aspiring to greater heights. A major distinction between how capitalism and communism function has to do with incentive to ascend to greater heights. Without that incentive, there would be significantly less growth and development in the society's infrastructure, which is a culmination of all the efforts, rewarded or not, made in the name of advancement. If the incentive were not there, the reaction would be to throw up ones arms in resignation, for after all, "what's the use?" Why knock yourself out if the rewards are to be the same as those who do not exert the requisite effort.

Occupational prestige most often determines where individuals are located in the social class structure. The positions in the structure are related to educational preparation and training. It is apparent that the placement of positions is not solely related to earning capacity. Over the years I have seen many charts, most listing Supreme Court Judge at the very top. In fact, this is the first to move physician to the top position. One conclusion that may be made in determining how and why the positions on the chart are ranked as they are has to do with the level of preparation required to attain the position. In almost all cases that means education. There are definitely inconsistencies to be found on the chart, for the positions are ranked in terms of the level of occupational prestige. Prestige is based upon the relative importance of the position to society, not to the individual. It is not difficult to see the importance of physicians and Supreme Court justices. But the inconsistencies may include such positions as garbage collector, street sweeper, and janitor. We could probably all agree that those positions are very important to society. We may have some difficulty in explaining why someone who "lives on public aid" would be listed above the five positions below him or her. Although physicians are thought to earn hefty salaries, that may or not be the case in every instance. Those working for HMO's often times are struggling financially. Would-be physicians in many cases cannot afford to practice their craft once they graduate from medical school. The high cost of the insurances they are required to have to practice are prohibitive to the point that, combined with the student loans some have taken out, they must find other occupations to do with their medical degrees. The physicians who are well compensated for their work are more likely to be specialists. Whether specialist or not, education is the mechanism for attaining the right to practice medicine.

To have an appreciation for the relative lack of importance of financial resources in gaining occupational prestige, consider the earning capacity of Supreme Court Justices. Prestige, again, is based on the importance of the position to the society. In cases such as Supreme Court Justices, society is not impressed with how much they earn. Society is more impressed with what they have done for us. The hope is that they are armed with the requisite qualification to render decisions that are equitable and that their decisions are constitutional. Supreme Court Justices earn an average of $209,000 per year. The average salary for the 26 top earning CEO's is $20, 000,000. The average salary for all CEO's is $167,000. And yet the prestige level for the top-earning executives may not compare with that of Supreme Court Justices and physicians. However, if earners are not concerned about prestige, they may be contented to "take the money and run." The question of educational attainment may not be the determining factor in their assigned positions. We could easily argue that our society is not one preoccupied with prestige. But we may be deluding ourselves. Witness the level of our preoccupation with not only acquiring things, but also displaying them. We are a society consumed with pretext.

The following is a brief vignette proffered by the author depicting his own experiences in grappling with the concept of social class:

> *Growing up in abject poverty in the Deep South gave me pause whenever the word "class' was mentioned. My limited understanding made me feel that "class" was synonymous with wealth. It was clear that my family, indeed my community, was as distant from anything resembling wealth as possible. Even as I developed some sense that there were gradations of wealth and "class," I was revolted by the thought that we, being poor, were considered unworthy. Therefore, "class" was a notion applied to an alien segment of the population. Now that I was beginning to understand that there is a distinctive group, of which we were members, called the lower class, the whole class system became repugnant to me, and I attempted to dismiss the entire concept. Silly me.*
>
> *Social class is extremely important in American society. Only Italy and the United Kingdom have lower possibilities of social mobility than the United States. We weigh the value and worth of individuals on the basis of what appears to be their socioeconomic standing. Eventually, it became necessary for me to face the facts and admit that ours is a very stratified society. How could I have ever thought otherwise? In adulthood certain questions have continued to gnaw at me. Why have some of my close acquaintances had much more affluent lives for themselves and their families? Were they more industrious? Were they more intelligent? Were they visionaries who could see beyond their very noses? What made the difference? In a much more mature and stable stage of my life I have concluded, without rationalizing, that the difference is totally unimportant. What is important is the extent to which one is contented in his or her own space, which means being aptly provided for and fulfilled in one's daily pursuits. But the question is vexing from a sociological perspective, and, yes, there appear to be some logical explanations. One explanation is that the cultures in which many were reared were quite different. I try to recall, without success, any young people in my environment who were from professional families. Failing in that, I attempt to imagine even the possibility of a discussion regarding investments in stocks and bonds. Such discussions were totally alien to my world. Where do young people get the notion that entrepreneurship is a solid possibility? Or that anything is more important than a steady job, albeit a low-paying one? Such ideas have to be born in one's environment and are often spread in social circles. Poor people cannot afford to take chances with their meager resources, for if they are not successful, they are left with nothing. Granted, those who do have discretionary resources, stand to lose it all as well. But having other important capital, such as educational backgrounds and broader training, offers a far better chance of recovering. The old adage "Nothing ventured, nothing gained" does not compute with those hanging on by their fingertips.*

I am fortunate with a good life in my middle-class status. My acquaintances, who are mostly tennis friends of more than twenty-five years, range all over the terrain in affluence and formal education backgrounds. We are all doing well, some a lot better than others. If we were to split hairs, we'd see that some are doing extremely well and others share my status, which is mainte- nance level. But I have learned a few things about stereotyping people based on preconceived popular notions regarding an individual's social, economic, and political persuasions. In our group there are conservatives and a minority of us liberals. (By the way, I think the four avowed liberals hold our own pretty well in the mix). Out of our Saturday morning dialogues emanate some interesting revelations. Hardly anyone is totally of one orientation or another. People may be conservative or liberal in certain areas and not in others. And the popular belief that those who are doing well have no concern about those who are not is a fallacy, at least in this setting. The players are Doug Arnett, Gary Champlin, Jim Clark, Charlie Granville, Mark Kenny, Larry Lotito, Jim Moore, Arnie Purisch, Don Rickner (my doubles partner), Mark Scheele, Mike Sul- livan, Phil Wheeler, and a few others. Some examples of the good works that they do follow: I am very impressed with Granville's leadership commitment to a help organization called Servicing People In Need (SPIN) giving aid and rehabilitation to over 74,000 recipients; and Sullivan serv- ing as a member of Christians in Commerce, which recently provided equipment to bring water to the people of Uganda; and Champlin, who donates generously to charities in Orange County; and the many others who donate their time and energy to charitable causes in their community; and Rickner, who directs Saddleback College's Foundation, amassing incredible amounts of funds for the college, including scholarships for students. These acts are done without regard for political orientation or social class status. Of course, this is only one setting. But twenty-five years of familiarity with these good friends is ample time to get the picture.

Social class in the Victorian sense is often repugnant to some in contemporary U. S. culture, for it smacks of "stuffiness" and exclusionary. The class system is at the root of our capitalistic society where the accu- mulation of assets is the yardstick by which the worth of individuals is measured. When there is a ques- tion of the level of one's worth, it is not about one's compassion for or sensitivity to the plight of others. It is about what the bottom line would be if all of one's assets were dissolved and amalgamated, including the very gold in one's teeth. That constitutes one's worth. Our society touts itself as one of the most chari- table on earth, given the fact that we are in the best condition to be so. But much of what we are about is excelling at the expense of others. Our most impactful institutions adhere to that philosophy. Business, for example, subscribes to the principle that it is good practice to bury competition. Both consumers and vendors hope to take advantage of each other. Both hope to gain more than they provide. The principle of *Caveat Emptor* ever prevails. Let the buyer (and the vendor) beware. It is simple to argue that these are principles that make our world go round. In fact, as capitalism continues to dominate in the world's economy and as globalism spreads unrelentingly throughout other countries, even socialist ones are buying into this "new" principle. So, what begins on an international and national scale has crept into individuals' quest for the accumulation of assets at the expense of others. So, social class is developing in areas where heretofore it would not have been welcomed. For the United States, the prognosis for social classes indi- cates continuing vitality, which bodes well for a society consumed with growth and competition, but not necessarily so for the struggling masses.

Works Cited

Anderson, Ronald S., Sr. "Japanese Ed." *members.tripod.com*. N.p., n.d. Web. 3 Feb. 2014.

- - -. *Japan: Three Epochs of Modern Education*. Washington, D.C.: Office of Education, 1962. *ERIC*. Web. 9 Feb. 2014.

Appelbaum, Richard P., and William J. Chambliss. *Sociology*. 2nd ed. New York: Longman, 1997. Print.

Benokraitis, Nijple V. *SOC*. Belmont: Cengage, 2012. Print.

Bryjak, George J., and Michael P. Soroka. *Sociology*. Needham Heights: Allyn, 1997. Print.

Bureau of Labor Statistics. "The Editor;s Desk: Earnings by Educational Attainment and Sex, 1979 and 2002." *bls.gov*. U.S. Department of Labor, 23 Oct. 2003. Web. 16 Jan. 2014.

Chafetz, Janet Saltzman, and Anthony Gary Dworkin. *Female Revolution: Women's Movements in World and Historical Perspective*. Totowa: Rowman, 1986. Print.

CONSAD Research Group. *An Analysis of Reasons for the Disparity in Wages Between Men and Women*. Washington: U. S. Department of Labor, 2009. *consad.com*. Web. 9 Feb. 2014.

Cortwright, R., and E. W. Brice. "Adult Basic Education." *Handbook of Adult Education*. Ed. R. M. Smith, G. F. Aker, and J. R. Kidd. New York: Macmillan, 1970. 22. Print.

Durkeim, Emile. *Suicide: A Study in Sociology*. Trans. John A. Spaulding and George Simpson. New York: Free Press, 1966. Print.

Farley, John. *Sociology*. Englewood Cliffs: Prentice-Hall, 1990. Print.

Henslin, James M. *Sociology: A Down-to-Earth Approach*. 12th ed. Boston: Pearson, 2014. Print.

- - -. *Sociology: A Down-to-Earth Approach*. 11th ed. Boston: Pearson, 2012. Print.

James, Charles E., Sr. Foreward. *An Analysis of Reasons for the Disparity in Wages between Men and Women*. By CONSAD. *consad.com*. U.S. Department of Labor, 12 Jan. 2009. Web. 9 Feb. 2014.

Kendall, Diana. *Sociology in Our Times*. 9th ed. Belmont: Cengage, 2014. Print.

Kornblum, William, and Joseph Julian. *Social Problems*. 10th ed. Upper Saddle River: Prentice, 2001. Print.

Marcus, Edward E., and Robert J. Havighurst. "Education for the Aging." *Serving Personal and Community Needs Through Adult Education*. Ed. Edgar J. Boone et al. San Francisco: Jossey, 1980. 41–45. Print.

Martineau, Harriet. *Society in America*. New York: Doubleday, 1962. Print.

Min, Pyong Gap, ed. *Korean Americans in Asian Americans: Contemporary Trends and issues*. 2nd ed. Thousand Oaks: Sage, 2006. Print.

- - -. *Koreans' Immigration to the U.S.: History and Contemporary Trends*. NY: Queens College, 2011. Print.

Pearce, Diane. "The Feminization of Poverty: Women, Work, and Welfare." *Urban and Social Change Review (Winter-Spring)* 11.1/2 (1978): 28–36. *SocINDEX with Full Text*. Web. 7 Feb. 2014.

"The Rise of Asian Americans." *Pew Research Social and Demographic Trends*. Pew Research Center, 4 Apr. 2013. Web. 5 Feb. 2014.

Stockard, Jean. *Sociology: Discovering Society*. Belmont: Wadsworth, 1997. Print.

Weber, Max. *From Max Weber: Essays in Sociology*. Ed. and trans. Hans Gerth and C. Wright Mills. New York: Oxford U P, 1946. Print.

West, John R. *There Are Always Blue Skies*. 2nd ed. Dubuque: Kendall-Hunt, 2009. Print.

Yearbook of Immigration Statistics. 2009. Washington: Office of Immigration Statistics, 2009. Print.

Young, Whitney Moore. *Bartlett's Familiar Quotations*. 16th ed. Boston: Little Brown, 1992. Print.

Index

population of, 31, 32
    racial discrimination against, 31
Chinese Exclusion Act of 1882, 31, 35
Chinese immigration
    value of, to United States, 31–32
Civil Rights Act of 1964, 50
Civil Rights Act of 1988, 27
Civil rights movement, 14–15
Civil rights organizations, 19
"Common schools," concept of, 1, 2, 15
Comte, Auguste, 3
"Cooley's Looking-Glass Self," 17
Credential society, 23
Cultural change and education, 1
Cultural diffusion, 30
"Culture Lag," 1

D

Du Bois, W.E.B., 5, 19–20
    education of, 20
    experiences with racism, 19–20
Durkheim, Emile, 4

E

Earning capacity and educational attainment by sex, relationship between, 10–11
Earnings, gender-gap in, 8–9, 10–11
East Asians, 42
East Indians, 39–40
Education. *See also* American education system
    and aging population, 45–47
    and common schools, 15
    in defensive mode, 1
    definition of, 1, 2, 22
    denying women access to, 16
    impact on social groups, 15–16
    need for diversity in, 22
    "one-size-fits-all" syndrome, 22
    and politics, interdependence of, 49–50
    professional degrees, 16
    role in resource accumulation, 10
    role in social progression, 17
    and scholarships, 9

    significance in social mobility, 7, 9–10
    social change impact on, 1
    and social class, 51–52
    social factors influencing, 2
    teachers' expectations, 17
    uniformity issues related to, 22–23
    and universal schooling, 15
    for women, need for, 9
    and women's progression, 10
Educational institutions, vexing problem of, 1
Educational programs for older citizens, 46
Education Amendments Act of 1972, 9
English language skills, 21–23
"Ethnic cleansing," 16, 43
Ethnicity
    definition of, 13, 15, 42
    importance in society, 16
    influence, 17–18
    and race, intersection of, 44
    uniqueness of, 42–44
        majority group values, 42–43
Ethnocentrism, 23

F

Females in U.S. society. *See also* Gender equity issues; Women's status in society
    differential opportunities for, 8
    earnings vs. men's earnings, 10
    educational opportunities for. *See* Women's educational opportunities
    roles in United States, 8
    social status and mobility of, 7
    voting trends of, 50
    women's issues. *See* Women's issues
Female students, teachers' expectations from, 17
Filipino Americans, 38
    college education statistics, 25
    household income of, 33
    political orientation of, 34
Formal education, 7
    and acculturation, distinction between, 1, 2
    accumulation of resources and, 10
    acquisition of, 9

G

Gender equity issues, 7
  gender-gap in earnings, 8–9, 10–11, 13
  and women's movement, 7–8
"Gender tracking," 16
Globalism, 23
"Graying of America, The," 45, 47
"Group consensus" philosophy, 29
Group pride, 15

H

Hispanics
  definition of, 21
  2010 median household income of, 26
  over-representation among poor, 23–24
Historically Black Colleges and Universities
  (HBCUs), 21

I

IEPs. *See* Individualized Education Plans
Immigrants
  Chinese Americans. *See* Chinese Americans
  English language skills, 23
  Indian Americans. *See* Indian Americans
  Japanese Americans. *See* Japanese Americans
  Korean Americans. *See* Korean Americans
  from Mexico, 21–22
Immigration Act of 1965, 38
Indian Americans
  characteristics of, 41
  college education statistics, 25
  household income of, 33
  political orientation of, 34
Individualized Education Plans, 23
Informal education, 9
Institutions. *See also* Social institutions
  in American society, 5
  importance of, 5
Intergroup
  conflict, 18
  harmony, 43

J

Japan, education system in, 29
Japanese Americans, 25, 26
  college education statistics, 25
  culture of, 29
  discrimination against, 27
  education of, 28–29
  "group consensus" philosophy of, 29
  household income of, 33
  internment of, 27–28
  negative attitudes towards, 31
  political orientation of, 34
  restitution, 27
  segregation in education, 19
  values of, 30
Jefferson, Thomas, 15
Job opportunities, 23

K

Kitano, Harry H.L., 26–27
Korean Americans, 25
  characteristics of, 37
  college education statistics, 25
  household income of, 33
  political orientation of, 34
Korean immigration to U.S.
  during Accelerating Period, 36
  during Contemporary Immigration Period, 36
  during Intermediate Immigration Period, 35–36
  during Old Immigration Period, 35

L

Language
  and culture, family's attitudes about, 22
  implications of emersion in, 22
Latinos
  definition of, 21
  obstacle for, in job market, 23
  segregation in education, 19
League of United Latino American Citizens, 19
"Life Long Learning," 45–46
LULAC. *See* League of United Latino American
  Citizens

M

Male students, teachers' expectations from, 17
Mann, Horace, 15
Marshall, Thurgood, 19
Martineau, Harriet, 5
Marx, Karl, 4
Mendez case, 19
Mexican Americans, 21
Mix-aged classrooms, 46–47
Multiculturalism, 23, 43

N

NAACP. *See* National Association for the
    Advancement of Colored People
National Association for the Advancement of
    Colored People, 19
Native Americans
    poverty among, 14
    separatism preferred by, 14

O

Occupational prestige and social class, 52–53
Older citizens
    discriminating against, 45
    educational programs for, 46–47
    impediment to society responding to, 47
    and "Life Long Learning," 45–46
    myth regarding characteristics of, 46
    voting trends of, 49
"One-size-fits-all" syndrome, 22

P

Parker High School, 19
Pensionados, 38
Politics and education, interdependence of, 49–50
"Post-racism" society, 13
Post-war Japan, restructuring of education in, 30
Poverty, 14, 18
Protestantism and capitalism, parallel
    developments of, 4
Protestants, belief systems of, 4–5

Q

"Quota," 15

R

Race
    definition of, 13, 42
    and ethnicity, intersection of, 44
    influence, 17–18
    in U.S. society
        African Americans, 13–14
        Native Americans, 14
Racial discrimination, 13
Racial phenotypes, 13
Racism, 13–14, 17–18, 19, 31
Rodriguez, Richard
    school education of, 21
Roman Catholics, belief systems of, 4

S

"Scientific method" for sociology, 3
Sexism, 5, 7
Social activists, 5
Social change
    impact on American educational system, 1
    pervasive, 2
Social classes
    among African Americans, 13
    aspirations to progress, 51
    and capitalist class, 51
    and education, 51–52
    experiences in grappling with, 53–54
    and occupational prestige, 52–53
    significance of, 51
    and social conflict, 4
    in Victorian sense, 54
Social conflict
    and social classes, 4
    source of, 4
Social contact, 13
Social facts, 4
Social functionalism, 4